Manifesting

Unlock Your Full Potential With Law of Attraction and Third Eye Awakening

(How to Stop Wishing for Change and Manifest Success With Visualization)

Luke Hawkins

Published By **Jordan Levy**

Luke Hawkins

All Rights Reserved

Manifesting: Unlock Your Full Potential With Law of Attraction and Third Eye Awakening (How to Stop Wishing for Change and Manifest Success With Visualization)

ISBN 978-1-77485-578-2

No part of this guidebook shall be reproduced in any form without permission in writing from the publisher except in the case of brief quotations embodied in critical articles or reviews.

Legal & Disclaimer

The information contained in this ebook is not designed to replace or take the place of any form of medicine or professional medical advice. The information in this ebook has been provided for educational & entertainment purposes only.

The information contained in this book has been compiled from sources deemed reliable, and it is accurate to the best of the Author's knowledge; however, the Author cannot guarantee its accuracy and validity and cannot be held liable for any errors or omissions. Changes are periodically made to this book. You must consult your doctor or get professional medical advice before using any of the suggested remedies, techniques, or information in this book.

Upon using the information contained in this book, you agree to hold harmless the Author from and against any damages, costs, and expenses, including any legal fees potentially resulting from the application of any of the information provided by this guide. This disclaimer applies to any damages or injury caused by the use and application, whether directly or indirectly, of any advice or information presented, whether for breach of contract, tort, negligence, personal injury, criminal intent, or under any other cause of action.

You agree to accept all risks of using the information presented inside this book. You need to consult a professional medical practitioner in order to ensure you are both able and healthy enough to participate in this program.

Table of Contents

Chapter 1: We Are All Connected 1

Chapter 2: The Effects Of Negativity 7

Chapter 3: The Power Of Energy 15

Chapter 4: Gratefulness 25

Chapter 5: Simple Step-By–Step And Action Plan To Attract The Opposite Sexe Using The Powers Of Manifestation 34

Chapter 6: Law Of Attraction 44

Chapter 7: Creation 61

Chapter 8: The Power Of The Subconscious Mind 67

Chapter 9: What Is The Best And Most Simple Ways To Create What You Want? 80

Chapter 10: The Power Within Us 90

Chapter 11: Vibrations From The Universe 99

Chapter 12: Mindset 110

Chapter 13: Learning What You Want.. 121

Chapter 14: Delivery -- Your Faith & Being Available For It 133

Chapter 15: How To Overcome Fear And Turn It Into Strength 137

Chapter 16: Steps For Attracting Health Wealth And Relationships 150

Chapter 17: Get Rid Of Your Fears 158

Chapter 18: Death Is Inevitable............ 171

Conclusion 183

Chapter 1: We are All Connected

No matter where in the world you travel, you'll see someone you already know. And this person will know many others who know more people. Eventually, that circle will return to the person who knew you. The old saying "it is a small world" holds true. What if there were more to our connection than that? All of our bodies are made up energy. These include light, vibrations and frequency. We know that each person has an electrical current running through them. It can even be enough to cause shocks when someone walks on carpeting. As electrical beings, all of us are interconnected in the larger universe. We have never been taught to tap into the other side of our brains and are therefore unaware of this connection.

Because this is how we have been trained, we spend the majority our lives interfacing with people superficially. For the most part we believe in a greater being or power than ourselves. Sometimes, we might reach out through prayer or meditation to that power because that's what we've been taught. Teachers are the best teachers. At some point in life, we seek out new knowledge, learn new points and view things, and sometimes discover that what is known is not all there is. You are about to embark on a journey full of new knowledge and enlightenment.

We are all connected by the power that has made us. No matter what you call it, this power didn't create us. Instead, it turned its back on us and left us struggling in a world of chaos and despair. This power exists within us and around our minds. It is part of our unconscious and conscious thought. It has unlimited potential to make your life the life you always wanted. Once you have learned how to tap into your power, all it takes is thinking about your wants and needs. There are two correct ways to use this power. You must learn it and be wise about how you use it. Once you have the skills to make the changes you desire in your own life, you will start to see the benefits of the connections you make to the lives and people you meet.

Because we are connected, we are also connected to every power created. Just take a moment to observe your surroundings. Everything has a place and serves a purpose in the natural world. Nature does not waste anything. If it has served its purpose, it is either recycled or used to support another creation. This means that you, too, can be included in the natural cycle. Every action you take in this life will have an impact on others. You might not notice some of your actions, or they may not even be noticed by others. However, nature or other people will notice other actions. All of your actions are noticed by the power who made us. If you stop to think about these consequences on a molecular scale, it would disturb the mind to the point that inactivity. We as a race of humans don't consider our actions at such an intimate level of interaction. It is precisely this inability to consider our actions that can cause us most trouble when trying to feel connected with others and our surroundings. We can often rationalize what we perceive as miracles as accidental occurrences, fate or karma. We have been taught to believe that miracles cannot happen to everyone. Therefore, we are unable to comprehend the moment when one happens to us. We make it harder for miracles to come to us by not acknowledging a miracle and realizing that we are connected with everything in the universe.

It is through our very connection with this higher power that all things can happen in our lives, in our environment, and around the world in general. This higher power provides protection for the small toad and gentle butterfly without them having any worries about their existence. Nature is a place where animals don't worry about food and even their friendships. Unfortunately, humans can become consumed with worries and fears because they think about everything to death. They don't realize that there is a higher power who can give us the same kind of gifts as we need for our own existence. Even though we strive to have sufficient housing and adequate food, it is not enough. Sometimes, our struggle can lead us to believe we are better than we are. We need to stop thinking of ourselves as the reason we have any possessions. We are allowed to receive what we need by the grace of this higher force.

The immediate cry for help is heard when people lose everything due to natural disasters. There is an immediate feeling of oneness when people reach out to others to offer assistance or to assist another person. Most people wouldn't consider this an opportunity to restart. Perhaps this is how the universe is trying to reset people's future. Many people in these situations find something better than they thought. They also end up making major changes in their lives that they didn't want to do. Sometimes life gives us a push in the stomach and tells our hearts, "Hey! Let's just get over this mess!" This is where we normally begin to see oneness with other people. But you lose sight of the oneness that exists with the greater power and the universe. Why? Because it is programmed in us to believe only what we can see with our two eyes. It doesn't have to be visible. However, that is not true. Once you allow yourself to relax and accept that you can live in oneness, with the whole universe, it will be the little things that bring you the greatest life-altering miracles. It's then that magic happens and your dreams turn into reality.

Chapter 2: The Effects of Negativity

Negativity is bad for your health

Have you ever heard the expression "worrying yourself sick"? You may be wondering where it comes from. As I stated in the previous chapters, there is a strong link between the mind and your body. The mind mirrors the body's illness. The reverse is also true. When you live your life worrying and stressing out, you will eventually attract disease and illness to your body. It's well-known that stress is a killer.

Unfortunately, it is easy for people to fall into the negative thinking spiral. It's easy to whine, complain and not do anything about the problem you are trying to fix. You complain and whine until the thing that you are complaining about becomes everything you think about. This isn't good. What you think will influence your life. If you are only thinking about negative things, how can you expect to see more positive things? That's right. There are many things to be displeased about.

It's easy for people to believe that "life can be so difficult". People from all walks of life believe that life can be difficult and impossible to attain their goals. You can only make that true if this is your reality. It is possible for you to live the lifestyle you want and be the person you wish to be. You don't have to follow the advice of others. The most important thing to remember is that you can live your life how you want.

Let's examine some of the negative consequences of negative thinking. Positive thinking and joy, and laughter will help boost your immune system. However, being negative about yourself or the people around you will make it worse. It makes your immune system weaker and breaks down. It allows depression to take root, which can lead to isolation from your family and friends. This is why isolation can lead to depression, which in turn can lead to isolation.

Your negative thinking does more than just affect you. It also has a ripple effect on the people around. Your bad energy can also be a drag on their spirits. Ever spend time with someone that is always downering? Talking about all the troubles they are facing. It's almost like they aren't happy with anything no matter what happens around them. Are you ready to feel this way? Feeling miserable constantly and making everyone around you miserable? I'm sure not.

Focusing on the negatives and focusing on them can lead to stress. As stress builds, it becomes easier to find more stress. It's the same with your thought patterns. You can easily fall into a vicious cycle. When you see something bad happening, you think that "stuff like these always happens to me". And guess what? You start to see more of this. It becomes a self fulfilling prophecy. As you expect bad events to occur to you, they do!

Cortisol can be created in the body when stress builds up. The higher your cortisol levels, the worse your body feels. It can also lead to weight gain and the breakdown of your immune systems. Additionally, cortisol production increases if we have too many thoughts that make us feel stressed and low. Plus, it's more difficult to find positive thoughts and new memories when there is more cortisol. Our brains react to worrying thoughts and anxieties as if they were real dangers. The brain is unable to tell the difference between what is real and what is imagined. As you can see the brain cannot tell the difference between real and imagined things. The more we dwell on our anxieties, the more danger our bodies perceive. If it believes that, and releases stress hormones constantly, it can eventually cause severe harm to our bodies. It isn't a coincidence that obesity rates among millennia's are on the rise, as well as reports of poor mental wellbeing.

Negative thoughts can control our lives and make it harder to overcome. Sometimes it may seem impossible to overcome negative thoughts and feel happy. I can assure you it is possible. It's possible. I've done this before and you can, too. Simply take that first step. Negative thinking makes it difficult to love what you love. It wants us be alone and miserable, feeling helpless. It seems like we can't help listening to the voice in our heads telling "you can't".

Negativity is the Brain

Multiple studies have demonstrated that self-focused rumination, attention, and depression are strongly associated. It can make depression worse and hinder problem solving. Constantly focusing negative thoughts on yourself can worsen many of the problems you already face. You even create neural pathways that can alter your thinking. Negative thoughts and constant feeling of shame can have serious effects on your brain.

You may not be aware of the Placebo Effect. You know, that little phenomenon where you hear something and feel better. The human mind is extraordinarily powerful. However, the reverse can also be true. It's the Nocebo Effect. Harmful beliefs hurt your body. When you believe that your body is a failure you can easily become one. When you believe you're unattractive, you become unattractive. When you think you're sick you get sick.

You can worry yourself into ill health. But, isn't it possible? Wouldn't it be healthier for you, your health, and your happiness to focus on being healthy and happy. People who live the longest expect to live longer.

Imagination is everything. It is the preview to life's future attractions.

- Albert Einstein

Nothing is as it seems, unless we believe otherwise.

Shakespeare

"You are what your thoughts make you." But you also attract your most positive thoughts.

Finding the Negativity

It is important to understand the root cause of your negativity before you can make a change in your thoughts. What "bad thoughts" do you hold onto? Do you think you're too fat? You're a loser? Find where you are holding onto your negativity and remove it. It's okay to feel sad about the past relationships. Learn to let it go. It's okay to let go of worries about your bills, your house, and all the stuff we seem to be obsessed with. Don't worry. Just keep paying. It will vanish one day. Do something about it if you feel overweight, unattractive, or otherwise unhealthy. Get active, eat more healthily, and get out there to meet people. Improve your body image.

There's no need to make yourself miserable just because you have a few extra pounds or don't look as glamorous as Hollywood movie stars. It's all about that "I'll make it happy when x" mindset I discussed in chapter 1 This must be stopped. Don't wait until you are happy to start working towards your happiness. Not after you have thousands of dollars in your bank account, or if your perfect partner is available, or if your dream job is secured. If you don't have someone to love your life right now, then those things will never come. Even when you don't get everything you desire, you can still appreciate and be grateful. The most important thing is being content with what's available. You create a disconnect between your accomplishments and yourself by wishing for more. No matter how wonderful everything is, you will always desire more. If you take the time to appreciate all of life and find love and happiness, you will be able to avoid that disconnect. You'll find peace.

Chapter 3: The Power Of Energy

It is likely that you remember information about energy from high school science classes.

There are two types in the universe of energy: Positive and Negative.

As energy is constant throughout the universe, so too is energy. This means that all of the energy currently in existence is all that has ever existed, and all that will exist.

Wait! What about power plants, cars? What about all those things that generate electricity.

Yes, power plant create electricity. Solar panels do, too. However, solar panels don't produce energy. They transfer energy from one place to another. There are active and passive forms of energy. Passive energy is found in fossil fuels below the surface. The oil is still passive once it has been extracted, processed and made into gasoline. Once it's been added to your car's tank, it will move through the line into the engine's combustion room and the spark plug lights it. It then becomes active. This passive energy was converted to the power to move your vehicle.

Now this energy was converted into exhaust. The carbon dioxide in the atmosphere is called CO_2. It can then be used eventually by plants or trees.

Energy is constant. There are only 2 forms.

Imagine a battery. You'll see a sign with a plus (+) and minus(-) signs on it. The symbols stand for positive (+), or negative (-), polarity. Both are required for your device to be able to run on battery power. It is important to understand that polarity doesn't mean negative or positive energy. But, in some ways it is.

What happens if two magnets are taken, one positive and one negatively polarized (which is not energy). They attract one other, right? You can repel two magnets of the same polarity, right?

Energy is simply the opposite. Energy attracts energy. Negative energy attracts energy. Energy is always constant. Therefore, there will be the exact same amount of positive energies in the universe next year as today.

Someone will attract positive energy and someone else will attract negativity. It's only the foundations of life. Do you want negative energy to attract all the time, or do you prefer it?

You have seen the impact it has on your lifestyle and your mental outlook. It's not enjoyable, isn't it?

The power of being positive

You might have heard of the 'powerful power of positive thoughts'. It was created by professionals and life coaches to help their clients to change their outlook and see the positive in their lives.

It's simple: start thinking positively, even when it seems difficult, and all negative feelings will disappear. And positive things will begin happening for you.

Also, think positive and you'll become more positive. Add the laws to attraction to that and you will see that positive thoughts can result in positive energy. Your positive energy will attract more positivity and good fortune.

In the next chapter, we'll be looking at transforming electricity. However, before that happens, you must first understand something fundamental about energy.

They are misleading when they talk about how to transform energy. You cannot change the polarity or nature of energy, as it is a constant. However, you have the power to alter the energy you attract.

If your recent life has been filled with negative events, it's possible that you are attracting them. To make a change in your life, first you need to change yourself. You won't transform the energy around but will attract something else.

While this may seem confusing, trust me. It will all come together before the end this book, and you'll see exactly how to transform your life.

How energy can improve our lives.

I want to ask you to pause and think about your life. I want you find somewhere quiet where you can focus and be alone. I want to encourage you to unplug your phone and spend some uninterrupted, quality time just you.

Once you have that information, I invite you to go back and look at your life. Use a plain sheet of paper to begin to record all the happy moments. I am talking about truly happy. These are times when you weren't sure that anything could get better and you just couldn't wait for the days to end.

It could have been an idyllic summer, where you were young and surrounded by your best friends. It could have been your family vacation. Everyone was happy and laughing.

Write these memories down.

Now, let's think back. Can you recall times in your past when everything was not going according to plan? When you couldn't wait until the next day, week, season ended? No matter how hard you tried, nothing seemed right.

Keep these memories jotted down.

Now, try to think back to each of these events and to recall what happened before them. If you can correctly recall the events that occurred between those times in your life, then you'll see a pattern.

Things were pretty good before those wonderful memories. Your adult self might have called them "great", but your younger self may think they were mediocre.

Right? Things were sort of falling apart just before these bad times. While these issues might not be a problem to you now they could have been a major issue when you were young. Bad grades could mean you were penalized for lying to your parent or doing other things.

Some events or bad days led up to those horrible memories. They seemed like they were building up to that horrible time in your life.

You see a pattern? You should. If not, you must think deeper to uncover the correct memories. Be honest, it's true. A series of negative events happened right before the wheels seemed to fall off your life.

Don't allow death, serious illness and accidents to anyone you care about to be misunderstood. It's not just about the aspects of your daily life that you have no control over. You can't lose your loved one instantly because of the laws and attraction.

Every good and bad period in our lives is preceded by a series smaller positive or adverse events. You may have been popular in highschool, or an elite athlete, and everything seemed to be going smoothly for you. You were confident, assertive, and could do almost anything (see? The laws of attraction worked.

You then graduated. All your friends went to school or work, and you attended local colleges because you couldn't get scholarships to any of the top universities. You became less of a star player and lost confidence.

You made friends at dorms. However, you were surrounded by people similar to you. Your attitude changed. You changed.

You noticed that suddenly things were falling apart. Exams were difficult. You failed a class. You lost interest in the major that you had declared. You were dropped from the team. You got into an argument without reason.

One day, you sat in your car or dorm alone wondering why things had turned so rapidly. It was only a few years ago, when life was good and you didn't have any worries.

A change occurred. While it may have been minor, you focused on the issue and considered it a problem. Your thoughts began to change over time. You started to blame your parents, the teacher and the coach.

The more negative and angry you become, the more bad stuff seemed to happen. It's a vicious cycle that can make it more difficult to break.

That's energy. It will be drawn towards the same forces. So if you start thinking negatively (e.g. "I'm probably not going to get that job"), your mind will also be drawn to these same forces. There are just too many applicants. Negative events are more likely.

Positive thoughts don't always mean negative events.

It is important to surround yourself in the right form to attract the same energy.

It is because of this that you can create whatever you want and more if the laws are understood and used to your advantage.

Chapter 4: Gratefulness

I was taught as a child to be grateful for what I get. I didn't know that being grateful was not a forward-looking action. You're not making a wish for an event past, you're creating gratitude for it so you can get more in future. Gratitude shows the universe that gratitude is something you do. It allows you to feel grateful for what you have been given and it vibrates that you are grateful. Imagine you get a gift but aren't grateful. It isn't that you didn't feel appreciated, it is that the Universe has decided that the gift it gave you is no good for you, and that it will stop giving it to others. We'll be discussing ways to vibrate gratefulness in this chapter. This will allow you to expand your blessings even more than you could ever imagine.

Blessings are a part and parcel of life. Blessings can take on any religious meaning, but they can also be used to express the flow of wealth through every living soul. We can be so inawe of the bounty that we could receive, when it is not our right. It is the norm, and not an exception. It is part who we are and what we do in the hierarchy.

These blessings come in many different forms. The blessings we receive can be classified into two groups: blessings, and curses. Yes, it's true. Even though a curse appears to be an antithesis of blessings, they are nevertheless two sides of a single coin. This coin is different. Normally, a coin is presented in one of two ways. You can choose to receive the coin head up or head down. If you keep track over the years of receiving coins, you'll see that roughly fifty percent of those times will be the same. The remaining fifty percent will go in a different direction. Probability, statistics and math aren't just for the geeks at school.

The coin of possibility is one that has both a blessing side and a curse side. It is the currency in the universe. If the universe is willing to give you something, it will. The coin is yours to use as you wish. If you're observant, focused, and highly attentive, the coin is all that you need to extract the maximum amount of this universe's abundance.

This day-age offers us only limited opportunities. Things that come packaged in pretty ribbons are a curse. There are, however, dark curses, which we all know we'd be happier living without. None of this is true. The deeper the curse, it is better. If we are able get over it, these so-called curses can change our cellular levels and make us more ready for the next level.

There is no such thing called a bad curse. It is not because we are good people that we expect 'good things to happen to us. It doesn't matter how good you are, you don't need to be perfect to receive blessings. It's all about seeing it as it is.

And herein lies the problem. We have become so used to viewing things in terms if our laziness and end up seeing the curse side of every opportunity.

Or, we see the blessing side of the coin and take so many of the blessings that we eventually come to believe that it's not as good as it should be or that it doesn't deserve our gratitude. This is the idea of entitlement.

The two states that make up the language of universe are the state of gratitude and continuance to take something for granted.

If you are grateful, then it means that you tell the universe that more of what has been given to you. You should not assume that the universe will give you more of the same. Remember, the universe can only deal in one currency. This is why it gives you so much. This is the currency for opportunity. The opportunity that we just mentioned has two sides, blessing and curse. Once you've been granted the coin of chance, you need to put your efforts into making something of it. There is no service that delivers to your home. You will need to take the coin with yourself and go out into this world to make it work.

When you are grateful, you are being grateful for that coin. If you show ingratitude, the spigot slowly turns off and you block that coin. It will not let you have the coin and it will stop you from doing anything else.

It is a crime to complain about anything that causes you to lose your rightful share of the coin. It will stop eventually. Understanding the difference between complaining and wanting something better is key. You can have a car to get you to work even though it is old and worn out, but it still gets you there safely and reliably. That is a blessing. It is possible to want better. There is no genie that will just magically appear and drive the car for you.

In the end, you won't get more coins for being ungrateful, no matter what you do or how desperate you try to make it happen.

Take Opportunities for Granted

Then, there's the state where you take your chance for granted. We have so far described the coin as having one side representing a blessing and another side representing a curse. Both are good opportunities. But we tend to avoid one and seek the other. If we pass up opportunities that are disguised as curses we, like the saying goes, leave money on their table. Every hardship, every curse, any difficulty is a blessing that's greater than what we can bear. C.S. Lewis once said, "Hardships are often prepared ordinary people for a extraordinary journey." He was referring about the coin of opportunities' curse side.

What does all this have to do with taking things for granted. When you receive all the blessings available, it is natural to take them as granted. You will take blessing after blessing as it comes, just as you would take the rising and setting of the sun each morning.

Do you know what happens if you take these blessings as a given? Your soul can be blinded to certain blessings that you take as a given.

It's akin to taking for granted the smile of a family member or hearing the voices of children. After you have it for a while, it becomes second nature and you lose sight of it.

Can you see what happens if you are blinded by the many blessings you receive? Can you even imagine the moment when you don't see the coins? Be aware that you can only see the coins when you go to them. Also, if it isn't there or you believe it isn't there, you will think that you don't have anything to work with. It's the same as the butcher who doesn't possess meat to put on the market.

If you don't know what to do, you will have little to no motivation to make it happen.

Conversely, you might consider a stance which is not prone to taking things for granted. The result is usually gratitude and gratitude. If you take the time to be present and enjoy every moment of it, then you'll find that you can return the proud and loud voice of gratitude that will allow you to get more opportunities.

I often hear the church say that the person with most difficulties is the one God favors. It is quite accurate. However, one crucial point is overlooked. These difficulties don't make them worse. These are coins for opportunity. You are given the resources and tools to make things happen. Someone who is gifted with multiple challenges is definitely gifted. It does not matter if a person is given many blessings, as these are also opportunities. The difference is that we already have adapted to the blessing. The curse will require new muscle. We have to cultivate the things within us. It is difficult and seems so hard that it appears like a curse. Do you find the muscle pains that come with working out a curse? If you see it as a curse, then yes. But, if you wait for it, this seemingly curse can lead to the blessings of greater strength.

How we look at the coins can make a difference in how we use all the blessings. It's important not to take this for granted.

At this point, there is one caveat. Blessings don't mean you will get the consequences or repercussions that you deserve. A consequence for something you did not like is not a blessing. It is a reminder to not repeat the same mistake. You'll continue to learn from your mistakes. The two should not be confused.

Chapter 5: Simple Step-By-Step and Action Plan to Attract the Opposite Sexe Using The Powers Of Manifestation

Power of attraction can be used as an effective tool to attract the other sex. Are you looking to find out how to attract the interest of the opposite partner in just seven days? Then you should look at the following steps.

Step 1: Make a vision with your soulmate.

This could be done on the first day that you start to use the power and attraction. If you are looking for a partner, it's possible to see yourself as wealthy and rich just as you would with money. This is a step that doesn't require too much detail. It's best that you don't pay too much focus on minor details. Otherwise, your list will be too long and contain too many characteristics.

Keep in mind that there is no perfect person. You don't want to attract someone who just looks good. Attracting the opposite sexuality and love should be your primary goal. Do not be too picky about the person you envision.

Step 2 - Create a love dream board

Once you have established a clear vision in your mind of the person you wish to attract it is time to remind yourself what you are looking for. Dream boards are an integral part of the law, or power of attraction. These boards are usually composed of collages that include images with powerful messages. They can be used to remind you what you want.

If this is the case, you will need to find a wall space that can hold your board. This is the place to display images that will boost your belief that love is in your future. These pictures can be found in magazines and photos that you have taken. You can also create sketches and phrases that will help you attract the woman you want to be with.

Keep the collage somewhere you can see it several times daily. The collage should be bright and cheerful, as well as able to bring you joy.

Step 3- Attract love and live as if in love

By living your life as if it were true love, you can easily attract lasting and genuine love. It may be awkward at first to do this, but it is crucial in attracting love and romance. If you are still uncertain how to do this correctly, don't worry. A card can be sent to your loved one, saying "Happy Anniversary, my Love"

Apart from these small things, it's also a good idea to have an attitude that makes you feel loved. You might start listening and smiling more. You can also make some changes in your home to better suit the person you are looking for. It is important to create a romantic, welcoming space that reflects your commitment.

While you wait for your beloved, it's a good idea set aside a section of your home so that you can practice your visualizations and other law-of-attraction exercises. This will allow you to set aside some time for visualizations and exercises.

Step 4 -- Spread love

Be the one to spread love, no matter where it takes you. Remember that attraction works by attracting like. It's no surprise that your desire to attract the love of your life means you have to also be loving. There are many things that you can do to spread love, even small ones. The best thing you can to do is be kind to strangers.

This will spread love, and it will send out the message to the Universe that you are worthy to receive love back. By volunteering some of your time, you can send love vibes. Your goal is to attract magnetically the same compassion, loving kindness, thoughtfulness, and love that you desire.

Step 5 -- Remove physical obstacles

You need to take certain physical steps to clear your mind of any emotional and mental blocks that may hinder you from attracting the love of your dreams. Consider what might be holding you back from attracting a partner or a friend to your life. These things should be able to signal to someone else that you don't still have feelings for your former partner or that he/she still lives with you. Clothing, books, and objects you do not like are some examples.

If it is difficult to return items to your ex-partner, try to find other ways to use them. If you are unable to return the items to your partner, consider selling them online and donating the money to charity. You may also notice that certain items you hold dear are hard to part with. These include photos and letters from love.

If you have trouble tossing such items out or letting them be, then it might be worth considering reducing their influence on your desire and ability to attract love. You can do this by keeping them in an enclosed box that you can't easily see. You can then let go the past and look forward to the future with the new love of your life.

Step 6 – Search for an object with a strong connection to your current intentions

If you find an item that is immediately appealing to you, you will be able to think of the perfect person you are inviting into your life. Once you have selected the object, make it a goal to bring it with your wherever you go. To remind yourself of the new you, hold on to it.

Another tip is to keep the object close at your heart while you're doing creative visualization. It will remind you of your progress towards creating a love-filled and exciting relationship. If you desire to attract an intellectual and smart partner who shares your love of books, you might be able to hold a book in one's hand during your visualization sessions.

The 7-Day Action Plan

Taken into account the above-mentioned steps, here is a 7 day action plan that will guide you on your way to finding the opposite sex.

Day 1 – Visualize your soulmate.

Day 2: Make your dreamboard. It should be about Love - The Romantic Kind, Of Course.

Day 3 – Act as though you are already in a relationship.

Day 4: Show love and compassion to others.

Day 5: Remove all physical barriers and obstacles that might prevent you from loving your new partner.

Day 6: Locate an object which can be easily associated to your intention or desires.

Day 7: Keep working on the attraction and visualization processes and wait for your new true love.

This is a great way to get the opposite sex in a matter of days.

A Long-term Action Planning

It is best to do the 7-day (1-weeklong) action plan. But, you can also create one that covers a longer time period, from around 1-year to a 5-year. To create a long-term strategy plan, which can last from 1-5 years, the first thing you should do is determine your goal within that time frame.

You could, for instance, decide to make a resolution to change your body and get your desired body in one year. Your goal should be making yourself more attractive to whomever you want to attract. It is essential that you establish a solid fitness routine and continue to follow it for the entire year. You will then be able show off your physical and mental health after the first one year. It is so important to ensure that you attract your dream partner.

In the 5-year action plan your goal is to find a partner that you will be able to spend your entire lifetime with. To put it another way, if your goal for the 5-year plan is to make yourself physically and mentally attractive to your ideal spouse, and then attract him/her over the next few days/weeks, you should set a higher priority. Ex. Finally, you will tie the knot.

You should make it a habit to put down your 1-week and 1-year action plans. The long-term plan should be put in an envelope and sealed. Set a date when you will open the envelope. After a year, or five years, you might open the envelope to determine if you have achieved what you have written.

The great thing about these action plans is that you can use them as motivation to keep going with the steps and actions necessary to attract true love. The next chapter of the book will focus on creating a visual board that can be used in conjunction with your action program. When you put them together, you have a greater chance of finding the love of your dreams.

Chapter 6: Law Of Attraction

The Law of Attraction holds that "like attracts love." It is what you think and believe. So if you feel miserable in your relationship or are always promoted by your coworkers, your mind might be focused on the fact that you aren't worthy. Everything revolves about your thoughts. Concentrate your thoughts on what matters to you, and not what you don't have or want. Clarify and refine what you think to make your wishes come true. Avoid being too abstract and be exact with the details.

The reality of impossible is what you will see when you consider it. If you enjoy toxic people, you will eventually have relationships with them. Tolerance for bad guys can attract them into your life like bees. The other side of the coin is to send the universe your heart's desire for a man with positive energy. You attract good men seeking women like you.

This is why serendipitous meeting the right person can be described as serendipitous.

Fate can bring together two people at the same place. It does not necessarily follow that you should have the same beliefs and likes as your partner. It's important that you have core values, traits, and characteristics that complement one another. These characteristics are crucial to build a strong foundation, and keep the relationship going as it grows.

A. What is the Law of Attraction?

This belief states that thoughts attract and can bring about positive or adverse experiences in your daily life. It is based the belief in pure energy, which resonates the same way as the Universe's energy. Simply put, your "thoughts turn into things and become realities."

The Law of Attraction, even though it lacks a solid scientific basis, is wildly popular and widely-used to improve one's health, wealth and relationships. It can sometimes be regarded pseudoscience and is one of many fascinating concepts in the universe.

According to New Age philosophy all manifestations are the result your conscious and unconsciously thought. It also believes that all energy has specific frequencies, and that they act as magnets that attract the same frequency. This will bring you closer toward your desires.

Buddha's saying that "whatever you think, you will become" is a common belief that sparked interest in all of the followers, scholars, philosophers and leaders. Over the centuries, there have been many experiments and teachings based on this principle. Emerson and Shakespeare are examples of famous people who convey the Law of Attraction by their masterpieces.

Oprah Winning, Denzel Washington, and Jim Carrey are the most popular advocates of this law today. Oprah, media mogul is a big believer in the Law of Attraction. She also credits positive thinking for her success. She believes that your thinking is what creates your reality. This belief is what has allowed her to achieve extraordinary results and overcome obstacles on her way to her goals. Denzel, an American actor, director and producer, believes that the human intellect attracts things. Jim Carrey used Law of Attraction (the power of intention and visualization) to achieve success. He had a story to tell about how he created a check for his self and visualized it happening. He made his first $10million and became a star in the movie industry.

Jay Z and Steve Harvey were among others who believed the Law of Attraction was a powerful tool.

Actor-singer-producer Will Smith believes that "our thoughts, ideas, feelings, and dreams are the keys to access greatness." Singer and songwriter Lady Gaga revealed in an interview that everyone has a superstar within that is waiting to be released and utilized to attain success. She explained that she changed her beliefs and used positive affirmations and mantras to achieve her dream life. Arnold Schwarzenegger said during his early years in the showbiz that he was confident that he would be the "number two box office Hollywood star one-day." Jay-Z strongly believes everyone can make their own luck. So if you want something to happen and visualize it, then do it. Steve Harvey was a TV host and radio personality. The Law of Attraction helped him build a successful career, and a happy lifestyle. He believes every person is an attractor of the same energy from all the universe.

All of their testaments were filled with the astonishing power of Law of Attraction. It acts as an incredible force that can make the impossible possible. It is the force that unites people, groups or nations. It is responsible for LOVE, one of the most powerful emotions in the world. Love fuels attraction. Attraction without love is not possible. If you don't love someone, there won't be any deep attraction. And everything will have no bearing.

B. It's all about love.

The Law of Attraction continues to be in motion. It is constantly in motion, acting as a magnet to absorb billions of energies, linking them with the vast network of frequencies which make up the universe. The Law of Attraction works in the same way as other universal laws. It can help you transcend the infinite mysteries of all things. It is key to any kind and amount of change you would like to have in this lifetime, as well as manifesting the love you need to achieve your ultimate happiness.

Understanding how it works can help you have a happy, healthy life. It can instantly transform your relationships and financial health, as well your well-being. It is always in action, processing the energy you send into space.

Remember that you're the focal person of this whole process. You have great power to shape your life, both now and in the future. You can unleash the power and potential within yourself by learning this information.

You have the amazing power to change your life. It all starts when you accept the power of Law of Attraction.

It is important to keep your thoughts positive and avoid sending bad thoughts. According to the old saying, "Whatever your thoughts are, it will come." You can attract good and beneficial things if you keep your eyes on the positive. If you are focused on negativity or lack, you will attract many negative things that increase the insufficiency of your life. When you place your focus on the love, you'll receive plenty of it.

Here's how you do it:

The Law of Attraction is a 3-step process. Ask, Believe, Receive.

1. Ask for the things you desire. Make sure you're clear and specific if your goal is to receive what it is. Don't ask the universe for things you don't need. It will only recognize the energy that aligns with your wish. It doesn't interpret you message or make

decisions on your behalf. It only acts according to how often you send it. You will see positive results when you send out your wishes if you feel joyful, happy, grateful, thankful, and appreciative. The opposite of this will result in you feeling sad, depressed, anxious or bored.

Make sure you're intentional about the thoughts and feelings that you create in your brain. Be positive and absolute in your thinking. No ifs and buts are necessary to make sure you have the right thoughts. To prevent the universe from picking your negative thoughts up and sabotage the pursuit of true happiness you must delete all negativity. The universe responds only to positive vibrations. So make sure you are focusing on happy, healthy, and positive thoughts.

2. Believe that your wish will come true and follow through. Keep a positive outlook while you wait for what you want to happen. Never lose sight of the results. Believe in the

process. Put your 100% vote in the universe to grant your wish. No one knows exactly when this will occur, but you'll know when your soulmate arrives. While you wait for him, try to improve yourself and your relationships. Your day should be filled with positive energy. You can show your best qualities such as kindness, compassion, empathy, and compassion. Learn to be more compassionate with yourself, your loved ones, and your friends.

Continue to be positive, thinking, feeling, acting and believing positively. You can let go of any self-limiting beliefs or fears that may prevent you from experiencing happiness and abundance. To be worthy, desirable, capable, lovable, and to receive the best, believe in yourself. Be enough for who you are, and do what is necessary to make it happen.

3. Your wish will be granted by becoming a vibrational match. Love is the foundation of your soul. It fuels your needs and inspires you to pursue your goals. You must maintain

positive vibrational connections with the universe to ensure you receive all that you desire.

You must give your whole attention to your intention. It is essential to be positive and live with joy, gratitude, appreciation, and love everyday. Give thanks. Gratitude feeds the energy and vibrations you send out to all of the Universe. The Source is the source of the love you seek, so thank him for his gift.

Attract a loving, supportive partner by becoming what you want to become. Your soulmate is already here and you can send gratitude energy to accelerate the manifestation process. To match the vibrations in the universe, keep a positive and uplifting emotion. This will help you to feel the same feelings when you receive your wish. Be positive and think positive thoughts. Positive thoughts can bring about positive changes in your life.

Be quiet, and then focus your attention on yourself to become a vibrational match for your partner. Imagine the relationship you will have with him. Are you content, fulfilled, worried, hopeful, or skeptical? Negative feelings are a sign that you're not ready to build a relationship with the man of your dreams. It is important to feel positive and confident. Eliminate tension, doubts and other lower vibrational energies that could block manifestations.

C. What is the secret to its success?

If you are able to see your desires in your head, you can achieve them. This cliche is well-known and has been repeated many, many times. It proves the power of your mind. Your brain works 24 hours a day to keep you healthy. It generates ideas that are more creative and thoughts that reflect the emotions or desires you have.

Your present life is the result of your thoughts. If you look back at your life, there are many examples of how your wishes have come to pass. These events all occurred because you believe in their reality. Even if things aren't going your way, you will still see the results.

Remember that your wishes do not create miracles. It is YOUR THOUGHTS. It is about the alignment between these thoughts and your emotions. It doesn't matter if you only wish or let the universe do the rest. You need to make clear, powerful, and empowered intensions. You shouldn't just say "I hope he loves me." Be specific and say "I would like he to accept me as I AM and love me as I AM."

Your intense desire is the basis of The Law of Attraction. Be certain of what it is that you desire. Instead of simply wishing, you can say, "I want to live a better existence." What better life do you desire? While it is possible that the universe will do you favors and give you what you want, being clear about your goals can help you be more precise. If you are looking for a great boyfriend, then your intention should be "I wish a loving, loyal and generous boyfriend" or "I prefer a tall, dark and handsome boyfriend."

If you want the Law of Attraction to work for your benefit, concentrate your positive energy on your wish. You must not doubt that it will manifest in your world. Only one wish at a moment. Once you have learned how to empower your wish with positive thinking and how the Law of Attraction works, it is possible to take your game to the next level. You should be aware of what energy you put into it as it could attract similar energy that can change the quality of life and relationships.

The Law of Attraction is not able to classify your wishes as big or little. However, it will allow you to dream big in order for great outcomes. There are no limit to what you're able to do or desire. All that you send out to the vast universe is not wasted. They will be there at the right times. This natural law is within your reach so you can attract everything.

Finally, you must live up to what you have said. Being the person that you want to be is all about taking action. Being kind to yourself and others is the best way to attract a kind-hearted soul. Sharing your love with your closest friends and family will make you a loving, romantic man. Show kindness and patience to others who ask for your attention. By doing positive things, your self-esteem will increase. It will make it feel good, increasing the positive energy to support your desire and intention. It allows the Law of Attraction to work faster for your good, filtering out others who are not in line with your needs and seeking the perfect match.

D. The key of the law at attraction - Persistence

Once you've discovered the Law of Attraction power, you can use it in your everyday life to shape your future. To become more efficient, you must have keys. Persistence is one. This is the secret behind many outstanding people of history and present-day. They took responsibility for their lives and persevered to make it happen. They took control and regained control of the lives they wanted.

The exciting news that quantum physicists have discovered that the Law of Attraction is activated in the human brain and can make it an ally, is making it more popular. It's easy to tap into the magic of this law. But the trick is in how you believe and make it work.

It is not enough that you wish. You must also hold the thought close to your heart and visualize it becoming a reality. It is crucial to make intentional steps in the real world. Be persistent. Keep praying to bring it about. Positive action and prayers can be essential vitamins to sustain your intention.

Every thought and feeling you make at any one time becomes a request. The Universe responds with the same frequency to your requests, resulting in physical manifestations. You must be aware of what your thoughts, feelings, and words are. Your emotions, actions and words have a significant impact on your thoughts. So be careful about what you wish for, before, while, and after.

For a happy, lasting relationship with someone who fits in your life perfectly, it is important to persevere.

To think differently and positively in all circumstances

Reacting with positivity in every situation

The choice to live in positive emotions

Focusing on things that promote better interpersonal relationships

By choosing to act with intention to realize your dream relationship, you can become the person you are looking for.

Know that there will be a delay in seeing your wish manifest in the real world from the moment you send it out. Give up on your desire to control the universe. If you let go of all attachments and give up your wish, the Law of Attraction will manifest it.

It is your job to keep feeding your wish with positive thoughts. You must not entertain doubts or fears that this will happen. It is the only way to stop negative energy weakening the mysterious process on the higher frequency. Keep dreaming of your dream man, and your dream couple.

Chapter 7: Creation

You can make any idea, thought or dream come true. You can make your wishes come true when you remove all the obstacles and blocks that are holding you back from synchronizing with the universe. If you notice what happens to you and others, you can discover the Law of Manifestation. You know it's true. Now I'm going to show you the steps to make it happen. Practice is the key. To manifest something is to receive it in the real world. It is a gift. It is a gift, no matter how smart you are. You'll get more once you become more. Once you've got more, you need to share it with people who don't know how. You don't have to give them fish, but you can teach them how. It's one of the ways I give back to people after they have given me so much. I promise you, if you give more, you'll get more.

This book covers significant material. We looked at the fundamentals of the topic. Finally, we examined the structure to see if there was a logic to it all. The point you need to understand is that making your dreams a reality is not a simple process. It's not something you can do in a series of steps. This is not the same as a pudding recipe.

Your dreams can only be realized if you live a lifestyle which aligns all the skills. Thomas Edison made the lightbulb reality.

You might be asking how to manifest. It is obvious that you want to know how to manifest. But, after reading this book it's like asking a tuningfork how to play the note. It is possible to manifest your desires if you keep a set of rules. When you have a different mindset, if you tune your vibration and if life is lived well, then you will be able achieve everything you desire.

Because three things are likely to happen. This means your desires are not random and not fanciful. This will enable you to realize your true value and identify the things that are important to you. This is when you can manifest your true potential.

Second, you will find the energy to get the job done. You'll be able move any obstacle out of your way and overcome obstacles that might otherwise stop you from moving forward.

Finally, this level will allow you to create the perfect vibration all the time. Once you have reached this level, not only will you be able manifest consistently but you will also automatically attract the things you need. They will be available waiting for and right infront of you.

Manifesting is about making dreams come true, and living a meaningful life that is based on success.

I have some more words for those of you who are curious about how to manifest the new Porsche 911 or the new Gulfstream 650.

Achievement vs. Rewards

We can see the benefits of comforts and monetary gain as being fine. Nothing wrong with being motivated by the benefits of your achievement. Don't be ashamed of your accomplishments and don't think you're less for it. The book will show you that there is more to life than this.

Anyone with decent credit will qualify for a loan in order to purchase a Ferrari. Gulfstream even offers financing. Or, you could get a jet-time-share. What's so important about this? Focus on the achievement. The reward will always come. If you imagine the super-yacht or sports car that will be in your driveway, you are only imagining the rewards you desire.

Focusing your energies of manifestation on making one million dollars, ten million dollars, or even 100,000,000 per day is a way to create the vibration that produces power. If you can make 100 million dollars a day, all the toys that your heart desires will be at your fingertips.

One other thing is that you can focus on your reward and ask to get a yacht. What happens after the yacht is purchased? What happens if your only savings are enough to secure a loan, and the yacht is already in the Marina? What's next? There will be disappointment.

Instead, focus on the pursuit of success. The rewards will soon follow.

I'd like to end by reminding you of one final thing. The universe only grants you what your heart desires, so it can even be setbacks. You will manifest what you desire, even bad things. Negativity and negativity are the things you will manifest. You can even cause disasters. Negative thoughts can make bad things happen and it reinforces people's belief that bad stuff will happen. You need to be positive if you find yourself in a negative spiral. Reread Chapter 4 to find the skills you will need to become a positive thinker. If you believe in yourself and want to have something positive happen, then it will be easy to see that you can have the best life possible. It is what it is that you believe will be.

Chapter 8: The Power Of The Subconscious Mind

Personal change has to begin at the subconscious level. If it doesn't, it won't happen. It is possible to make a change in your thinking and live a happier life. You can use your subconscious to alter your mindset. All you have to do is plant the idea in your mind, and keep it there for a few minutes.

If you work on your subconscious, you'll likely be able to release the latent power within your subconscious mind. This will allow you to come up with new ways to get what it is you desire in the time and space you have. The law of attraction says that you should attract things, not chase them. The subconscious mind is what will make it happen.

Most people fail because even though they want to succeed, they are not able to express their desires clearly to the subconscious mind. Without knowing what you really want, you will not be able to drive the wheels of success.

How can we tune and awaken our subconscious minds to do what we want?

Make a visionboard.

You can create a graphic representation of your goals and hang it somewhere where you'll see them every day. This allows your subconscious mind to pick up and start vibrating the universe for your dream.

Just before you go to bed each night, write down your goals.

There is no better way of influencing your subconscious than to trigger or stimulate it just before going to bed.

Your brain works best when it is sleeping. Writing down your goals every night prior to bed will help you to saturate and align your mind with your goals.

How the Subconsciousmind Works

The subconscious mind can do more than you might think and is more powerful than we know. It is the engine of our bodies. It is the nerve center of memory, controls muscles, makes us work efficiently, and it also acts as the engine.

Think about it. Everything you do is controlled through your innermost minds. It learns from us and then assumes the responsibility of what we do. Imagine what this innermost mind could do for you to change your outlook, attract what is important, and bring you success.

How the Law of Attraction combines with Your Subconscious mind for Success

You already know the law that attracts is simple: what you think most is what it gets. This is because your subconscious mind, knowingly or unknowingly, is instructing you.

The subconscious mind is powerful. Therefore, we need to be able to tap into its power to gain success and advantage.

Positive thoughts will inspire your subconscious to send positive vibes. Success will follow. Our subconscious must be given instructions. It will then learn how to help us.

Your subconscious mind learns from repetition. Your subconscious mind will help you memorize, act, and react to more things. The subconscious can learn what we want from our memories, and we can communicate it through repeated vocalizations or thought.

Your subconscious will help you get there if you tell it repeatedly.

De-clutter your mind

Clear thinking demands clear thoughts. Unfocused thinking will lead to a mind that is distracted and on edge.

There are many ways you can unclutter and free up your brain.

Write it down.

There are many things that happen in a person's brain. Therefore, you don't have to store everything in the brain. Make sure you have a tool that helps you write everything down. This tool can be used as a type of storage device that allows you to save any information that you might need. Take a notepad or mark your calendar if you have an appointment. A journal can be a more detailed record. A journal helps you release any tensions, such relationship issues, and gives you peace of head.

Don't keep any memories of the past.

We should get rid of all the memories we hold on to, including those that have led us astray, past mistakes and missed opportunities. These memories are what most people hold on to and refuses to let go. Memories that bring about sadness can cloud your thoughts and keep you from focusing.

Avoid multi-tasking.

Take on one task at a time. Start with the most important. Then work your way down the list. You will then dedicate a certain amount of time to organizing everything.

Ensure your mind is clear during this time and remove all distractions from your task.

Take control of the information you consume.

Too much information can lead to brain fog. This information, which you get every day through reading magazines, newspapers or watching TV, surfing the web, and accessing social networking sites must be controlled.

You can limit your access to information by controlling how much time you spend on social networks and other information sources. Unsubscribe to online magazines or blogs that don't provide any value. Respect the opinions and disregard irrelevant information.

Make a routine.

Create a routine in your life for everything. This will help to reduce the stress that your brain experiences.

Prioritize.

There are so many tasks that you need do every day. You cannot do it all. Keep a running list of the most important tasks and work with them. It will give you the mental space and time you need to be clear.

Mental clutter is a blockage of our inner thoughts that can get in the way of clear thinking. Get rid of any unnecessary thoughts and clutter in your head that do not contribute to clarity or value.

Nurture Your Artistic Side

You may have ever felt your mind is full of thoughts and not knowing what to do next. This feeling is very common in a world filled with multiple responsibilities.

Arts are an excellent source of creative thinking and can be very useful in controlling and managing your thoughts. Particularly visual arts such as drawing and writing can be very helpful in achieving clear thinking.

Writing is cathartic. It helps you to coordinate your thoughts. You can clear your mind and reduce clutter by writing three handwritten articles each day.

Clear thinking can be achieved by recording how you feel. Also, note why you feel that way. And what you intend to do about this feeling. You'll be able look back on your writing and feel accomplished.

This trick often helps you to throw your thoughts away. Write down all the issues that bother you and then crumble your paper to throw them away. Research shows that people who throw away their worries on paper are less likely care about them.

Drawing is another way you can express your feelings. You don't need to be an incredible artist. All you need are a piece if paper and some crayons. Drawing is an effective tool that can help you focus and clear your thoughts.

Nurturing your artistic side can have many benefits

Art stimulates creativity.

You can write free-form, or you can advance a plot. Writing keeps your creative juices going. By connecting your thoughts and logic, you are able create new ideas.

Writing can help you organize ideas and make them tangible. Writing challenges you to think in new ways to convey this information to readers.

Creative art reduces stress.

It is possible to have clarity of thinking when you are totally immersed into 'the creative zone.' This meditation can calm your mind and make you feel relaxed. Painting and drawing are relaxing hobbies that leave you feeling calm and clear.

Art provides a distraction to your brain, which can help you get rid of negative thoughts. Leonardo da Vinci states that painting includes all the ten functions associated with the eye, which include light and darkness, location, shape, color and the body, closeness and separation, motion and rest.

Enhances self-esteem.

Art boosts concentration, drive, and focus. It helps you think for the long-term and to resist impulses. Creative art allows hormones to send dopamine, also called the "motivational molecule", which stimulates neurons and alerts brains for learning.

Drawing and writing have been found to be effective tools to improve clear thinking. You don't need to be an excellent writer or artist. To relieve stress or calm your mind, you can simply take a piece a paper and draw or write your thoughts.

Get Your Blood Pumping

Regular exercise is an excellent way to improve mental clarity and relaxation. Regular physical exercise has many health benefits.

Regular exercise can reduce stress. It allows you to experience mental calmness and serenity. Mental calm is the perfect condition for clear thought and thought processing.

For mental relaxation and mental relief, aerobic exercise like running, jogging, skipping and cycling are the best. These exercises will improve your mood, boost your energy and concentration, as well as relax your mind and body. The body's ability to sweat helps it release beneficial body hormones which aid in relaxation.

Exercise is also a great complement to other areas that can improve your overall health. Exercise is a great way to improve your overall health. For clear and mental mental clarity, it is important to have good physical health. Mental illness can distract you from your ability to think clearly.

You can exercise from almost any place you have space. You don't even need to go to a fitness center to exercise. You don't have to be a runner if you feel stressed out or tired. This will boost your happiness and mood by increasing your endorphin levels.

Exercise boosts your mood. It also strengthens your mental and physical health, which makes it easier to deal with mental pressures. Exercise regularly can lower your risk of stress-related illnesses.

Do you feel stressed out from work? You'll be amazed at the results of exercising. Exercises release brain hormones that promote happiness and prevent the development of memory-deadening diseases like Alzheimer's.

Both exercise and relaxation will help you reduce stress and improve your mental health. It is important to choose exercises that are not too strenuous for you. Research your options and consult experts before choosing the right exercise program.

Being active will allow you to think clearly, eliminate stress, and live a more fulfilled and happier life. Do light exercises now before you begin more strenuous workouts. You'll wonder why you didn't exercise sooner. It's important that you reap the rewards and are able to think clearly.

Chapter 9: What is the Best and Most Simple Ways to Create What You Want?

The Law of Attraction focuses on manifestation methods. According to this law, everything you desire is yours. This means that "like attracts love" It is easy to overlook the Law of Attraction's power, seeing as you will constantly come across it.

In order to manifest your dreams and achieve your goals, you must keep your thoughts and beliefs positive every day. After that, you can let the universe take care of everything else.

The Law of Attraction can be applied to all situations. The universe will fulfill your desires if you concentrate on what you want and envision them. The universe doesn't just know what you want. It needs to be active in bringing your desires into reality.

The manifestation techniques focus on what you can do to quickly boost your positive energy. To make manifestation work, you must have strong beliefs, a great wish, and overflowing gratitude thoughts. All negative feelings, including doubt and disbelief can cause manifestation to fail.

These are the easiest and most powerful ways to manifest your wishes, not in any particular order.

1. Focus on positive thoughts, positive emotions and positive thinking

For you to manifest positive energy, your thoughts must be focused on your desire. Your energy must flow with the same frequency as you think. The energy should have the same vision and love, passion, affection, as you. This will allow it to produce excitement and fondness in your body, mind,, and soul.

It is important to have a clear, specific mission. Only then can the universe understand you and fulfil your desires. Don't confuse your universe. Keep an open mind, give your all and be positive. Then, you'll find plenty of opportunities.

Your manifestation drive may be hindered by your past thoughts or worrying over events that haven't happened. It's because past thoughts are often a source of regret, anxiety and other negative charges. It is possible to manifest your goals faster by focusing your attention on the moment.

However, this is a very important reminder. Watch your thoughts. Negative thoughts can cause you to manifest, which can make you feel worse. Be gentle and love yourself to defeat the negative thoughts in your mind.

You can overcome these unsettling emotions by looking at an inspirational self-reminder.

"Don't talk negatively about yourself. Your body can't tell a difference. Words can be powerful and spellbind; this is why spelling has been called. Your perception of yourself is important. By changing your perception of yourself, you can change the course of your life. Bruce Lee

2. Visualization's Power

The visualization techniques stimulate both the LOA, as well as your subconscious. These methods are used by everyday people, celebrities, as well as athletes from all walks of life. This method must be practiced daily in order for you to realize your dreams. It is best that you practice visualization at night one hour before bed. Why? Do you know why? The subconscious mind can't tell the difference between them. Instead, it absorbs the last message from the conscious mind and programs it into the subconscious. The subconscious brain then reacts to the message and makes it tangible.

It's easy to practice visualization. Visualization is very easy. Choose a quiet area without distractions. Sit comfortably and open your eyes. Imagine you are in the theatre, watching as you perform in a movie. However, you can choose to do whatever suits your preferences. Remember, our brains can be creative and potent. If you can focus on your goals and feel confident in yourself, then the universe will grant them. Clearly define the results you want. This is the time to visualise your end result.

Imagine your dream car. You will need to know the model, type, color, capacity, interior and exterior details. To get a sense of the car, go to the showroom. You can also google the car's specifications for an image. From there you can print out the specifications and images of the car. Then you can paste it in a place where you can easily see it or save it to your phone and computer.

I admire people who apply visualization techniques to their daily lives. This motivates me and many others around the globe.

Jim Carey had a vision of directors interested in him before he became a famed actor. He also used to imagine people he trusted telling him, "I love your work." Today, Carey has become a Canadian-American actor. It's amazing.

Muhammad Ali, an American professional-boxer, credits visualization techniques for his success. Ali used visualization techniques to imagine himself winning a fight in front crowds. Amazing story!

Muhammad Ali said, 'The man who lacks imagination has no wings.

3. Trust the Universe and believe that you deserve it

To attract the best things into your life, you need to love and be kind to yourself. If you are serious about what it is that you desire, you can manifest. This feeling will serve as a platform for communication with the universe. The universe will then bring you abundance in order to fulfill your dreams.

Your heart should be open. Let the flame in your soul burn and you will feel the positive emotions rushing through your body. This will make your dreams come true faster than you ever imagined.

4. Cultivate gratitude

Gratitude is one of my favorite topics because so much in the world today lacks it. Consider the people you surround yourself with: family, friends and strangers. How many people do you show gratitude for? How often do I hear people say, "Thank you", "I value", "you have been kind", "I admire" etc. It could be in one day, one week or your entire life.

Gratitude will attract the LOA. Kindness and gratitude will rejuvenate your manifestation journey and bring you more abundance. It's a beautiful act that will bring joy to your heart.

Grit can help you transform your mindset from one of insufficiency and into one that is full of joy. To achieve this, channel your energy to focus on what you already have and not on what you don't. Be positive from the beginning to help you focus your long term energy positively.

Write a Gratitude Journal daily. This is an effective practice that has been tested. You can start a journal to record five things you're grateful for every single day. You can then read what you have written and internalize the positive feelings. All negative feelings will be gone soon.

5. Kindness

In all religions and cultures, kindness is a valuable virtue that is respected and valued by everyone. Kindness is the act or behavior of showing kindness to others. Kindness begins within you with positive and loving feelings. This is followed by compassion towards others and gratitude.

"Continued kindness can do much. Kindness can make mistrust, misunderstanding, and hostility disappear just as the sun makes ice melting.

Quoted By Albert Schweitzer

6. Smile

With your smile, be sincere and generous. When people see you smiling and you smile back, they will naturally smile back at your smile. This will make everyone happy, you and them, instantly.

7. Vision boards

A vision board is a visual representation of your goals. It can be made digitally or manually. Use images and text to express your ideas on your vision boards. Make it fun.

Vision boards are very effective. Vision boards are very effective. They can be filled with pictures and motivational words that will help you visualize better and encourage you to work harder towards your goals. The best place to keep your visionboard is somewhere you can glance at every day. It's a great way to feel like you've achieved your goals and then visualize what you want to do next.

8. Manifestation affirmations

If you wish to manifest, use positive statements and present tense. Your subconscious mind will remember to receive only positive messages and you should manifest as if your dreams have already come true. Once you have said the affirmation of positivity, you must trust the universe to provide exactly what it desires. The declaration should be clear and concise. Write it down, go over it daily, feel it, do it, and most importantly, have fun.

Chapter 10: The Power Within Us

Is it possible to see the beauty in this world and not find flaws? There is an explanation for everything you see, taste or hear on this earth. Everything works together in perfect harmony. From the capacities and state of our bodies to tiny critters who have a reason to be there, everything works in perfect harmony. We are able to live on the sun's surface, with enough light from the moon. What can we do to think that God has made this world unreal? Nothing is beyond the realm of possibility. The world we live in is perfectly and completely possible for everyone.

How could I possibly say such a thing when some of you are born into poverty and others are brought up in monetary wealth? Because The Law of Attraction was incorporated into the universe, this statement is true. According to The Law of Attraction, everyone on Earth has the potential to make their lives as good as possible. It doesn't make any difference where you were born or how wealthy your family is, and regardless of whether you have been accepted at school or if there are no legs or arms, it doesn't matter. The Law of Attraction is the same that brought everyone into the world.

There are some things that we can't alter. If you were born into this world without legs or arms, it is not possible to simply develop them. In any case, those who were born into similar circumstances to this can currently take advantage what he's been given. The Law of Attraction enables us, on the whole, to have the life we always desired. The Law of Attraction will help you to make your life easier. This is the key of survival. The Law of Attraction might be considered a hypothesis by some. This is completely wrong. The Law of Attraction can be compared to The Law of Gravity or The Law of Relativity. It is also a proven Universal law that we cannot resist.

The Law of Attraction tells us that our thoughts, emotions, and actions can influence the outcomes of events, situations, and people that happen to our lives. This means we can do, be, and become whatever we choose by utilizing our positive considerations. On the flip side, this is impossible within the all-inclusive laws. The converse is also true. We also create all our adverse conditions, mainly by the thoughts we have and the feelings that we express to The Universe. This isn't just a thought. This is a universal law that all people live by. It is not unlike any other all-inclusive laws. It is impossible to escape it and it is unlikely that it will evolve. It is the fact that it really is. The Law of Attraction differs from all others in one way. The Law of Attraction - the unrivalled all-encompassing law that can be controlled We live within a web of Cause-and-effect. Every idea or feeling we have has an impact.

There are two ways in which we can make use of our considerations. The first is that they can be used wildly without any awareness of the effects it will have on our thoughts and emotions. Another alternative is to learn how to control emotions so that they do not limit the positive outcomes in our lives. The Law of Attraction operates in the same manner as all other general laws. Once we learn how these guidelines function, we can benefit from this law and have the life we desire.

The Law of Attraction is something that many people seek to understand in order get more money. The Law of Attraction has many benefits. It can help you in every area of your life. After you have read this book, I encourage that you take advantage of The Law of Attraction. Put it to work in all areas of life. It's your ticket to financial prosperity. However, it is not enough to be financially successful. It can be used for getting the things you want but it can also be used to help you become who you really are.

I will explain how The Law of Attraction works throughout this book. I will also share with you specific ways to use The Law of Attraction in a way that is efficient and effective. My goal is for you to create the reality you desire.

I'd like to first share my story about how I learned about The Law of Attraction. Because they might be useful to you, I included this story along with other interesting stories related to LOA. These accounts will help to give you a better understanding of The Law of Attraction.

This story is the perfect example. The truth is that I intuitively used The Law of Attraction in my life to attract The Law of Attraction. I thought I was in constant contact with God. I had been communicating with God every day since the discovery of The Law of Attraction. I believed that I had an inexplicable connection with Him. Our relationship was complete. I didn't know then that my relationship could have been much deeper than that. What I didn't know was that God needed me most often to have a conversation with Him. Although I was grateful to have certain things, I wasn't always grateful for all the good in my life.

I see the value in this since my relationship with God was not what I expected or could have been. However, my genuine gratitude towards God for what He gave me was valid and genuine. It just went on up to now. I was grateful that God made things work out for me, but I forgot to appreciate His blessings when things did not go according to plan. I didn't reprove God for the problems, but I would ignore the blessings that I have at the moment.

Retrospectively, it's no surprise that when I was 35 years old, something felt missing from my life. I was blessed with an incredible husband, three adorable little girls, and a home that was comfortable. I had everything I needed to feel fulfilled. I felt that there was more out in the world that could bring me greater fulfillment.

It was something I considered missing back then. While I believed in God growing up, I didn't have any faith and I certainly did not go to church as a kid. I tried visiting many churches in my adult years, but none of them felt right for me or my family. One day, someone knocked on my door. Jehovah's witnesses came knocking again, this being the second time that these two ladies have visited my home.

If it were my husband, I would have answered the door for these wonderful people. I, on my part, am very open-minded. I will usually spare a few minutes to listen to what they have. I knew I did not want the Jehovah's Witness lifestyle. I don't share their beliefs, and sometimes we had our little debates over what my bible says and what I believe. I held strong beliefs I believed in that were right and good. Although I thought I was living ethically, I knew there was something missing. I had my own little chat with them that day. Looking back, it was a great thing that I answered my husband's door that day. My life has been forever changed after a brief chat with these two ladies. If you're curious if Jehovah's witnesses is something I have done, the answer to that question is no. I explained that

I wasn't sure what religion I was looking to find, but that it wasn't Jehovah's Witness.

Then, one of the ladies said to my face, "Ask God!" Ask Him about what it is that you are searching for. He will tell you. Okay, okay, she didn't say "ask God." She said, "ask Jehovah." So, I said, "alright, I will." When the two ladies left me, I did just that. God asked me, "Lord. What am I missing in my life?" What is religion? If so, which religion is best for you? Please help me find what I'm looking for. For 3 days I asked God the same question several times a daily. I would ask Him the same question each day. It wasn't always the same exact words, but it was the same. I was then on Netflix for the fourth time. Guess what I found! The movie, "The Secret." After I saw The Secret, I knew it was the answer I was searching for. God had answered the prayer. I watched the film over-and-over. It was unbelievable to me that such a simple concept could be the secret to my success in life. I was desperate to learn more, so I read books about The Law of Attraction. This was exactly what was needed. It wasn't religion. It was simply a new way of life. It was a positive attitude, a way of living and thinking that allowed you to enjoy your life to its fullest. It was not just prayer - it was a way of building an extraordinary bond with God (or any higher being) so that I could understand Him back when He spoke to me.

No, I'm normal and I don't hear voices. Yes, I can get a little crazy from time to time, but not as much as my husband. It's an entirely different way to hear and understand God.

Chapter 11: Vibrations from the Universe

You are responsible for three things that are often misunderstood. The first one is the thoughts that you have. The second is the inspirations or feelings you receive. Your brain/mind creates your thoughts. Your inspirations are vibrations from the universe you feel deep in your heart but are very silent. Your body generates primal instincts which give rise to the feelings that you get. Each of these must be functioning well and correctly interpreted. The best gifts you receive from the universe in the form if feelings. We usually confuse them with the emotions generated by our louder bodies.

Differentiating Inspiration from Learning

Do you meditate? If not then you should reevaluate the strategy of your life and your pursuit for success. If you don't meditate, you may be missing key elements that will help you achieve a better result with a lesser effort. Also, it is highly probable that meditating is not something you do. If you don't meditate, you're likely to be constantly frustrated by failures.

Two ways to be successful in life are possible. Either you accept the consequences of failure as a guide, or you can seek the answers you need.

Don't get me wrong. Failure isn't necessarily bad. It can also be the best teacher. It is there for you to learn the secrets of life so that you are able to aim for what you want.

Meditation is a way to connect with the Universe

Meditation is a different approach. Meditation prepares your mind to listen to the whispers around you and make the right choice when it comes time for you take a decision. You instinctively know what you should do in every situation.

Meditation is the most powerful and effective practice a person could do. There may be reasons for some people to leave the meditation school of thought. Meditation is neither spiritual nor religious. It can be spiritual or religious if you wish.

Meditation can be considered a force that brings peace to conflicting systems of mind and body. The willful will of the body will always seem to follow one direction, while that of the mind will always be completely opposite. We can give in to the temptation of one or the opposite and feel a disorienting sense of guilt. But the constant debate between these two ideas can be chaotic, distracting, and even dangerous. Meditation helps you to unify your systems and create harmony between the scattered voices. This eliminates distraction and brings about peace.

You've probably experienced the chaos and conflict of reaching for a smoke 12 hours after quitting. The conflict between your "body" that craves nicotine and the mind that has decided to quit, or the desire to get a sports car is what drives the battle. One side wants to be behind the wheel. While the other side says that you should save your money so you can buy the best car you can afford.

Each person has had to deal with many opposing forces over their lifetime. Sometimes we cave to one force, and other times we fight for the other. Whatever decision we make in life, the future will be shaped by that choice. You are on the right path to one set, and you can break your promise not to smoke. We've all been there.

As you observe these fights and chaos, you will notice a third player on the battlefield. He is a silent umpire. It's called a conscience. Some call it the heart. These words, however, carry significant baggage which can distract from the discussion on meditation and success. We'll refer to it now as our core. To begin, you must identify what we call the body, and what is called the mind.

A lot of what we perceive of the world is based on our senses. We sense what we see, hear, feel, and smell. Each of these senses is not enough to translate into anything. Our senses do not communicate anything. They are simply sending electrochemical messages to our brains. It is our brain which interprets the information. It doesn't matter if it is sight, sounds, or smell. If we don't have any previous introduction, we wont be able to see or sense what we are seeing. Non-binary data is sensed through association.

Binary data is data which can only be one or both of the above. True or false, yes or not, on or offline, right or wrong. There are no shades, or in-betweens, of gray. At the beginning, only one of these binary processing options was available to the central nervous. But as humans evolved, our thinking patterns and thoughts became more complex. It even enabled us to predict future events based upon present circumstances. As the brain develops the mind, and the mindsets that are built on it, it becomes more powerful. This observation could be applied to ourselves. If we were to learn more about ourselves, our consciousness would return to us and we would be able ask the questions that will elevate our existence. This higher level thought is absolutely amazing.

However, the ancient part in our brain still speaks the truth, even though it is hidden at the base. Fear comes from the fear of the unknown. Fear is a powerful primal emotion that evolved to defend themselves from predators. That fear can still haunt us today and disrupt our entire thought process as well as the outcomes.

You can conquer fear by learning how to tap into the inner part of your soul.

Understanding the book's ultimate purpose is essential as you travel this book. This book is about making yourself the best possible. This book is all you need to regain your power. It's about showing you how to access unlimited potential and understanding. This book is about awakening. It is about showing the world that there is a teacher inside of you that you can tap into. Asking for what you need will bring you back to the source.

Meditation is not just about lighting candles and closing the eyes. Meditation is not about lighting candles and closing your eyes. Silence is not an ineffective tool; in fact silence is one of our most powerful resources. If you can tap into that power, all you need, the greatness of your imagination, the power you crave are yours.

The path to success consists of three steps. It is this path that must be learned and mastered if your goals are to elevate your potential and bring you to the top in your lifetime.

The first step in mindfulness development and implementation is the second. The second is the practice of focus. The final step is meditation at various levels.

When you master these steps, there's nothing you won't be able do.

Fourth Dimension

Normal humans are limited by the past, present, or future time modules. He can only see the surface of his conscious life. Past and future are only a part of the imagination of the higher mind. All-time modules exist within a context of a complete past. He can return to the present and look ahead, foreshadowing tomorrow.

The fourth dimension encompasses the integration of present, future, and past within a particular frame. The fourth dimension of the relationship with higher self is possible because your physical existence will not allow you to see the future, past, or present in the same way.

The three-dimensional physical world we live in is the fourth dimension. We are part of that fourth dimension. It isn't in our physical bodies, but rather it is related to the soul or the subconscious. To experience the presence of the fourth dimension, it is necessary that you link the conscious and unconscious parts. It is the link between our brains (brains) and our souls. The fourth dimension enhances the impact of inspiration, knowledge and spirituality on one's life.

A conscious connection between brain and soul creates a mindful connection which connects the conscious with the subconscious. It eventually takes the fourth dimensions to a conscious level where it is possible to feel it. The fourth dimension is a realm of conscience that celebrates the importance and value of happiness, harmony and righteousness. Fourth-dimensional thought brings you closer and more in touch with your divine self. It enlightens, inspires, and allows you to express your greatness.

Your highest form is manifested when you are in a higher consciousness. You receive inspiration or creative ideas. It may appear as inspiration, or a creative concept. Inspiration can come from their higher part. This inspires all who are looking for energy, vision clarity, enthusiasm, people and resources. Fourth-dimensional thinking plays a vital role in expression. It is possible to manifest from a higher consciousness and allow everything to come to you according to your deepest self. It is possible to see the many benefits of expanding your consciousness and understanding one's relationships as part of the whole of life.

Tips to awaken a fourth dimension

Everything that exists in this fourth dimension is beyond our physical reality. These are some ways to develop a quadrangular mindset.

*Be a observer. Be open to any possibility. You can see the whole picture.

*Learn the art of letting go of the need for something.

*Ask for what your heart desires. Seek the inner light, the meaning of life, and divinity.

*Pay attention always to the core. Your soul is always looking for experience. However, your physical mind desires material. The essence of the item is what you need.

As consciousness opens up, the third-dimensional refined thinking appears limited and meaningless. Everyone can feel angry or outraged at those who spread the word. In the fourth dimension the reverse is true. However, there are fewer physical judgments. Spirituality is the subject matter in every situation. It is essential to awaken your conscience for this.

Chapter 12: Mindset

We must overcome our negative attitudes toward abundance in order to receive the blessings and gifts of the universe. This is because our subconscious minds can block us from moving forward. I was listening to Tom Hopkins, a sales Guru, give a talk many years back. He used an example of his speaking at a realty conference to highlight the power of the subconscious. He asked a woman in the front row, if she was feeling fine because her appearance was not good. He began to present, but she quickly dismissed the question. She later confirmed that her health was good and continued. A few minutes later, he asked the same question and suggested that she looked a little pale. He asked her the same question again and she confirmed she was fine. She thanked him for his concern. This continued for several more times (6 to 7 total), until she finally admitted that she was feeling rather sick. His main point was to emphasize that our subconscious minds have the ability to make us believe almost anything we ask. This is exactly the way we have acted when it comes down to our negative attitude towards abundance.

One day, we all have experienced something in our lives. It could be from childhood. We were taught something that makes us believe we aren't worthy. Instead of being focused upon financial abundance, many people become focused on poverty. If we realize that we can break this cycle through the power of suggestion, then surely we should be doing this instead of focusing our energies on poverty and need. We've covered all the emotions associated with this mindset. But I'd like to add a few more. These emotions include feelings of guilt and a desire to blame others for our situation. This thinking creates a selffulfilling prophecy.

The green-eyed monster called jealousy can make us fixated on everyone else's better fortunes than ours. Playing the victim is the best way to get everyone to help you and to feel sorry for the burdens that you are carrying. This victim mentality is usually accompanied with a feeling depressed and the fear that nothing will change. It is obvious that all the feelings being discussed here are not positive. Therefore, the universe will take action on these feelings. It centers on the vibrations relating to hopelessness, depression, envy, jealousy, anger and sadness. This negative emotion can cause you to become physically ill, stress out, or even suffer from chronic illnesses such as depression.

If you are a victim of a negative mentality, the only way to overcome it is to be as free from them as possible. Below are some tips.

How to change your mindset

* First, realize that your current mentality is not serving you in the right direction to create abundance in all areas of your life. It's preventing you and your family from making the right decisions to help them achieve wealth, prosperity, happiness, and

abundance. While I don't think this will be easy, you can change your mindset and outlook to prosperity, wealth, abundance and success with some effort.

* The second step involves changing the language you use in order to avoid referring to the lack or money. Positive affirmations will help you to have more abundance than lack. We'll be going through some fantastic affirmations in a bit that will help you with this. If you continue to focus on not enough, it can be like playing the victim. Always ask yourself this question when you think about mindset. You might be surprised to find out that it is subconsciously. However, the goal is not to make things worse.

* Next, your attitude towards abundance and wealth. Begin to see abundance as an opportunity for growth, learning and experiencing new things. It is time to replace jealousy and worry (or that nervous knot in your stomach when you hear someone refer to money). Joy and gratitude will replace the

feelings of jealousy and anxiety. We'll explore gratitude in more detail down the road.

* Daily practice the art of meditation. You must practice. It takes time for you to let go of the noises and clutter in your mind so that you can live in the now. This can be done by getting creative, taking time to connect with nature and painting. You can also learn to play a music instrument. Each of these actions will help you change your negative thinking. Julia Cameron's book, "The Artist's Way; A Spiritual Path to Higher Creativity," (1992) is a bestseller. She recommends two things that will help you declutter your mind and allow for creativity to flow. 1. Write three pages of random note freehand every morning (yes... And, 2. It's easy to set up a weekly artist's date with yourself. They will be able to help you move out of any negative spaces within 12 weeks. You should remember that I didn't claim it would be simple. Some of these negative, limiting beliefs have been around for many, many decades. Breaking this cycle will require time and effort.

* Next, you should break down your goals into small, achievable steps. You will feel less overwhelmed when you face a mountain of obstacles. Every step you take toward your goals is a victory. Make small, achievable goals you believe you can achieve. Once you're done, reward yourself. This will keep you focused and motivated to continue moving forward.

* Learn to pay attention to what your body is telling to you. It is important to take time out to rest and rejuvenate your body and mind when you feel stressed and tired. Even something as simple as a stroll on the beach with your partner or taking a relaxing bubble bath by candlelight can make a big difference in your energy levels. Be aware that anxiety, stress and depression all negatively impact the vibration of the universe. Make every effort to remove these emotions from your life as quickly as you can.

* Being accountable for where you are now is one of the most crucial parts of changing your

mindset. You can't put the past behind you. All the excuses we can find. We must learn from our past choices and be able take responsibility. You already have access to this information, so you can get more information and tools to help achieve what you want.

Your Conscious and Subconscious Mind

Wayne Dyer discusses in his book, Wishes Fulfilled: MasteringThe Art of Manifesting (2012) the various roles our subconscious mind and conscious play in shaping and molding how we live our lives. To make things second-nature to us or become a habit, first we have to learn the basics on a conscious and subconscious level. Then, once these skills are established, we can call upon them for help even decades later. Take a look back at the time you first learned to bike. It took a lot more effort to balance, steer correctly, maintain the proper motion of your feet, and put tension on both pedals in the correct direction. Although it may have been many years since you last rode one, I can assure you that your body would be able to remember everything if you tried it again.

You don't necessarily have to learn everything on your own. There are some things we learn at birth that form many of the beliefs, habits, and routines that we carry around with our lives.

Some of Dr. Wayne Dyer's statistics can be quite astonishing. I think once we begin to see the role that our conscious selves play, we will understand just how essential it is for us all to be able consciously to wish for everything that we desire. Our conscious mind controls only 4 to 5 percent of all we do. This includes everything that manifests into our lives.

If our conscious brain is only responsible to a small fraction of everything that we attract into the lives of others, then it follows that the remainder of 95 to 96 percent is what is manifested in our lives due to the subconscious thoughts we have formed.

If we want to improve the circumstances of our lives, then we need the ability to alter the way our subconscious mind influences almost everything we do. We should also work to become more aware of some things that we do. Many of our thoughts, actions and behaviors result from operating completely on the subconscious autopilot' point. Although this is good for many areas of our lives it can also be detrimental. We need to question whether subconscious autopilot actually works in our favor.

The subconscious mind of the human body never goes to sleep. However, it does continue working when we actually fall asleep.

"The unconsciousness or sleep is the normal state" - Neville Goddard

Wayne Dyer stresses the importance of this state and suggests that within the five minutes prior to falling asleep, we should concentrate on asking the universe all the questions we need. Your subconscious mind will create the same conditions when you wake up as it was before you go to sleep. This is one reason why subconscious programming with positive beliefs or desires is so important.

"The measure and extent of what you do in the waking three-thirds is determined by how much consciousness you have when you go back to sleep. Except for the inability to feel that you already are that which you desire or that you have it, there is nothing stopping you from achieving your objective. If you feel that you have achieved your goal, your subconscious will allow your subconscious to manifest your wishes. ~ Neville Goddard

This begs the question whether you should be using powerful affirmations that will bring financial abundance, well-being, or any other kind of abundance into your life right before going to sleep at night. Neville Goddard says that when we sleep, our conscious beliefs can be altered to create the life we desire. This advice is found in Chapter 7. I suggest you review this advice before you head to sleep. Identify a few important affirmations that will help you raise your vibrational frequency with the universe.

Chapter 13: Learning What You Want

You've likely started to envision what manifestation looks like and how the law of attraction works. The problem that many people have is not knowing their goals. If you don't know how to manifest it, you won't be able to make things happen. Even worse, you may be feeling like "I don't really know" when you ask what you want to eat. Do you often stare at your closet in a state of uncertainty about what you will wear?

When you say "I do not know", you create an environment where you don't. It doesn't matter what the words mean. As you've seen, your words create reality. This means you might not know what your goals are or how to make them happen. I bet that you already know what it is. Even though you know it deep down, you aren't ready to admit it.

All those thoughts, dreams and hopes that you have pushed aside because they aren't possible or can't happen are what you need to be bringing into the world. They are signals from God to you that this should be your life. That is what you are going to do. Think about all the things you have been unable to let go of and then decide what you would like to create from them. It's possible to manifest all of them, but for now let's just focus on one.

A Plan of Action

Action plans are what you need to make your dreams come true. It is essential that you are able to give life legs to your dreams. While the Universe won't give you all the answers, it will provide the means to achieve your goals. Let's discuss the best method to create an Action Plan.

A visual representation is possible

In your action plan, the first thing you should do is create a visual representation (or a mindmap) of your goals. Clear communication about your goals is essential to accomplish this. The next step is to break down the goals into manageable pieces. These smaller goals should be SMART goals. This stands for specific measurable, actionable and time-sensitive. This lets you know exactly when your goal has been achieved. Let's look at creating a Mindmap.

First, in the middle, write down your "Why." This is your ultimate goal, what you are trying to achieve. This could include traveling all over the world or staying in luxury hotels. You can list up five things in your "why?" section. This should link to your life purpose. It is better to stick with "whys," which work together. Instead of trying to list all career options, such as money, health and job, try focusing on health or just money.

Below that, write your rewards. These are the items you will be able to receive once you have achieved your goals. You can make these rewards as big and small as you like. One reward might be a trip on a luxury cruise. It could also be a smaller reward, such as a visit to the spa or a movie. Next to your rewards you should make a note of when you'd like to see those things. This could be in a few short years, a few long months, or something else.

Next, trace four diagonal lines from your why. The top is where you will write your "three years goals." The middle is where you will write your "lifetime goals." And the bottom is where your "three months goals."

In the section for "lifetime dreams", list all your goals. A lot of people will include financial abundance. Others will add that having a multimillion pound business is a great goal. You can list all the things you want in your life in the long-term. If you want to be financially wealthy, I advise you to write it that way. Many people like to write out what they want to do to become financially free. Free should be used to describe things you want to get rid. As an example, say you want to be completely debt-free. You should also say you want to be financially prosperous. Suggesting that you want financially abundant sounds like you don't really want money.

Once you have completed your "three years goals," you can then move on to the next step: breaking down your big dreams into smaller goals. Now, take a look at your "lifetime goal" list and consider what is attainable in three years. This could be the ability to start a business. Other passive income streams are possible. Your first book could be yours. List the things you know that you can accomplish in three years so you can be closer to your ultimate goal.

Next, take your three-year goals and break them down to make them smaller. What can a single year do to help you reach your three-year goals more easily? This could be a promotion. Losing weight. Building a stronger relationship with a boss/co-worker.

Next, you'll set your three-month goals. These are things you can achieve in three months that will bring you close to your 1-year goals. This could include learning more about yourself and reading a book. You may also consider returning to school if your primary goal calls for more education.

Now you have a map and can move on to the next step of creating an action program.

Create a visual representation to represent your daily routine

Next, you can focus on the smaller components of your overall goal. This is how you can create a daily action program to ensure you're always working towards your goals. This will make it easier for you to stay on track and will help you get things done.

Place your "oneyear goals" on a piece of new paper. Take a look at your second mindmap to see what was in that section. These are the lines you need to draw again. The top left line is "strategy." The top right is the "daily plan." Bottom left is the "daily feeling-good plan." Bottomright is the "daily habits".

You will need to write your strategy to reach your one-year goals for "strategy". This could be returning to school, taking extra classes or strengthening your relationships at work. It might also include daily relaxation and exercising.

Two lines should be drawn from this and one must be labeled "skills" and another "mentors". The strategy will work if you have these two areas. You could choose to mentor someone you know, or someone who is an authority figure that you respect. Your chosen field of work will dictate the skills required.

On the "daily focused" page, you will list what you would love to do every day. This could be writing in your gratitude journal, taking care of your emotions, working on something, and so forth.

Also, add two lines to this section. This should be labeled as "top actions" or "mindset". Under "top actions", you will list the three things which you will do every single day. In "mindset", write your mindset goals like patience, compassion, positivity and the like.

Now, look at your "daily good plant". These are things that you do each day that make you feel good. These could include exercising, meditating, reward systems, and other things that can relax you. The most important thing is not to include alcohol or drugs. A glass of wine can be a good thing, but not if it causes you to feel distressed. It is possible to have a glass of wine with your bubble bath. But the bubbles are what will help you relax and not the wine. Problems can arise when you turn to addictive pleasures to make yourself feel better.

The last section is for "daily practices". These are activities you're going to make a habit out of every day. These might include reading a good book, affirmations, time with your family, visualizations of success, and other activities.

Now, let us move to step three.

Develop a monthly action program

We've moved from macro to micro. Now we will be looking at the middle. Before you start planning out your monthly plan, make sure you look back at the one-year goals. This is what should you be striving for.

First, identify your next month's goal. Sit down and imagine yourself reaching that goal. Then, feel grateful for your accomplishment. Then, create a reward system for yourself when you reach your monthly goal.

Next, write down the actions and intentions you'll need to take to maintain your positive emotions and keep you feeling good. Next, you will need to list all the habits or skills that are important for that month.

Next, create a second list of goals that you would like you to reach in this month. It is important to reward each goal.

Next, choose the five most important actions that will help you reach your goals. Concentrate on the 20% tasks that will yield you the 80% results. You can use a blank planner to record these important events, reminders, appointments, and meetings for the month.

We will continue to work on this and then move onto the weekly schedule.

Get a Weekly Planning Plan

We're making things smaller. This will ensure that your weekly goals are being met. When planning for your week, be sure to review your one-year goals.

Write down your goals for the week. Now, imagine yourself reaching that goal. And then feel thankful for it. Imagine the reward that you will receive for reaching that goal.

Next, write down all the things you're going to do throughout the week. Then, write down your weekly to-dos. When you are done, sort your tasks by priority. Then, visualize yourself effortlessly and efficiently completing each task.

Next, come up with your own personal to-do lists for the coming week. Make sure they are in order of priority. Imagine yourself effortlessly completing each task. The week will be a time to track all new habits and goals that you have for the month. Make a list of the things you did, when they were done, how many times, and how long.

Take a notepad and record your daily goal. Picture yourself reaching these goals. Feel grateful that you have. Next, list your three most important priorities every day. Make sure to write down your law of attraction quotes each week.

As you'll see, rewards are mentioned several times throughout this section. When learning and achieving new knowledge or behaviors, the human brain will respond to reward and feedback. If you want to improve your performance, it is necessary to ask for feedback. Rewarding yourself for reaching goals can keep you motivated.

Chapter 14: Delivery -- Your Faith & Being Available For It

As we mentioned in relation to the law o f attraction and manifesting, how quickly your manifestation arrives or if it arrives at all is all dependent upon your unwavering faith that it's possible. You can manifest whatever you desire if it is something you truly believe in. There is no possible way you could not. This is because if your beliefs are fully embraced, then you can align your daily actions with them.

Getting Rich -- Prosperity Consciousness

"Prosperity consciousness" is what rich people possess. This means they view money differently than average 'worker bees'. They see money as leverage - an exchange for energy. Money is simply energy. Most people exchange time/effort (energy), in order to get money. Highly successful wealthy people see it entirely differently. They think about how to use the money and other resources they have to create value and make more money.

Even if your business is not for you, there's no reason to think at this level. However you must believe another belief rich people have about money. That is, that it is unlimited. This belief will help you leverage the law and attract more money to you life.

The law of attraction will attract energy and excitement to you by making money seem abundant. Remember, the law is not intelligent enough to know exactly how you feel. It will only be able to determine if you are feeling positive or down.

Prosperity consciousness is therefore about having a positive attitude about money. It's about knowing that you can attract money and opportunity by feeling good about the subject.

Being Ready For It

Millionaire lottery winners go bankrupt. This is a common occurrence. It is because they are not ready to take advantage of the tremendous wealth that has been presented to them. They spend, invest, and then spend with no idea of how to use the opportunity presented to them. Your life may not be prepared to receive the life you desire. To be ready, I mean that you should have the knowledge and infrastructure to make it happen.

Let's try a realistic example. Let's assume you would like to be able to afford the dream home you have always longed for. If you do not plan out your beach home well, the likelihood of it coming to fruition is lower. It is at this point that the visionboard and the POV visualization are extremely important. You can visualize the home you want in your head before the money appears. This will help you know the steps to follow to obtain the beach house. You will already know which house you want. All this is a way to help you manifest money and the law-of-attraction.

Like you prepare your home to welcome a newborn child, you should prepare your life to allow for the manifestation of money and the things that you plan to spend it on. It is possible to bridge the gap.

Chapter 15: How to overcome Fear and Turn It Into Strength

One thing is sure: Fear can not be overcome with reason.

These logics will help you channel your emotional energy in a positive way to avoid panic attacks.

This guide will teach you how to transform fear and fear into strength. It also includes a short, practical exercise to open the mind and conquer any fear.

Fear: enemy or ally

Fear, especially when linked to real risk, is a primary emotion.

Fear that is suppressed or denied can cause you and others to underestimate the dangers. Fear may also be overestimated, which can lead to panic and panic.

It would be extremely harmful to try and eliminate fear from our lives beyond the possible.

If you can see her in a friend that comes to your aid then she will become your valuable ally. You can also use her energy to benefit.

However, this can be difficult because fear is a powerful emotion. It can sometimes cause trouble. It is because anxiety and panic disorders are so prevalent in our society.

How can you avoid panic?

How to transform fear into courage

To answer these questions, it is essential to first understand:

How does fear triggers our mind (and body)?

What are some of the most common unconsciously committed mistakes?

You can win the panic when you let fear take control.

How to overcome panic attacks

Our mind is programmed to foresee and anticipate possible dangers. This automatic mechanism's function is to protect us, and ensure our survival.

This is why the mind, when it's not trained, constantly generates negative thoughts and worries. Sometimes, they can even be catastrophic.

The problem is when these thoughts become true and you fear the physical sensations.

Fear is actually a physiological reaction that triggers in our bodies a response that predisposes us in the face of danger to attack or escape. This adrenaline rush enables us to react quickly in order to defend ourselves or escape from danger.

The problem is, that often the dangers we encounter in everyday life are not real. They result from negative thoughts that foresee or anticipate imminent danger.

In certain cases, panic sets in suddenly. Our inner world is trying send us a message. Perhaps our inner world is trying to tell us to act on a change we are holding off on, to listen more to an unmet need, or to fulfill a suppressed wish.

Coronavirus is a time of fear: What to do when the enemy appears?

Being in an emergency situation, such as we are currently experiencing, makes it difficult to overcome fear. External factors make it difficult for one to escape or defend himself by fighting.

In this instance, you might feel strong anxiety and helplessness, which could lead to a blockage or conditioning of the mind that can make it difficult for you to live your daily life peacefully.

It is important that you understand the emotional reactions that are initiated in order to soothe anxiety or to counter the negative thoughts that can fuel anxiety.

These dysfunctional reactions often lead to control and repression.

Here's how you can recognize the most common mistakes so that they are avoided and fear transformed into inner strength.

Controlling this will cause you to lose control

The first mistake when one is scared of their feelings is to do control rituals with an intention of alleviating anxiety and fear.

These reactions are not controllable because they are spontaneous and you may end up exacerbating their symptoms.

This is how they can be controlled. This is what turns fear into panic.

How to deal fear of disease or hypochondria

Even if you are motivated to act, impulse actions can have devastating consequences and make things more complicated.

For example, fear of illness can lead to the search of the internet for potential diagnoses of any symptom. This feeds the fear, which in turn causes panic and can cause the mind to become overwhelmed with worries.

These risks can create a stress-induced state and psychological tension which can weaken the immune response.

The bad thing about fear is that it can lead to the realization of your goals.

Even with the best intentions, you can get the worst results.

Warum is this all happening?

Is it possible that these unhealthy behaviors can be stopped?

Understanding the next step is a great way to open your mind up and direct it towards constructive action.

How to control emotional reactions.

You can face your fears with awareness.

Our minds tend to place emphasis on the immediate danger, not the longer-term threat.

Therefore, when you experience strong emotions, your instinctive responses to anxiety are likely to be impulsive. They can be more rational and powerful than your own will.

Emotions can actually be found in different places in your brain. These emotions are far more primitive and immediate then the complex processes associated with rational thought.

This is how one might act impulsively, which can lead to a worsening of the situation.

This is the root cause of impulsive, automatic emotional reactions. When emotions take over, we don't think about what the consequences are.

Awareness is the only weapon that can defuse impulsive reactions

It is possible to avoid emotional reactions that could lead to more harm by thinking about the future.

You can overcome fear by turning it to courage

The paralyzing belief that it is impossible, that it is too difficult, or that it is not possible for you, can make it seem overwhelming.

This limiting belief can lead to the worst outcome: blocking any action against an unpleasant circumstance, and possibly even passively suffering it.

Only by seeing fear in its face can we confront it and learn to control it.

If we refuse to acknowledge it, denial or repress it, we run the risk of fear leading us to places we do not want.

Fear can be the engine for change.

Fear, rather than desire, can motivate us to take the necessary steps to bring about positive change.

The only way out is to channel your fear-based energy towards strategic and productive actions.

Fear can be a distraction.

You can make your fears stronger by contrasting them with your attempts to suppress them, escape or escape. Accepting them and facing them, amplifying your strengths, will make them stronger.

How to overcome your worst fear in just 2 steps

How to confront your biggest fear

This exercise is easy to do whenever you feel anxious, fearful, worried, or panicky. But, I recommend you do it now to enjoy its "pleasant" effects.

First, face your fear.

Sit down comfortably and take 5-10 minutes to think about the worst fear you have.

What is the thought or fantasy that triggers it?

Begin to imagine your worst nightmare. You will never be disappointed. You can imagine every detail like you are in a film.

Don't reject it, but instead look at its face. Pay attention to it.

Do you feel the energy and fear in your body.

Take a moment to feel the sensation.

Instead of rejecting the feeling, try increasing it. It's like turning up the volume.

Keep your eyes closed and focus on your worst fantasy.

This exercise works best if you do it for 30 minutes. You can also start it by starting with 5 minutes.

Step two: Use your imagination and channel your energy.

Was there anything you were able to see?

Is this the real risk? Are the possible dangers overexaggerated in your mind, making them seem almost exaggerated now?

If you think the risk may be real or imminent, then ask yourself the following questions:

What should I do (or don't do) if I want to make the worst of my fears come true?

Make a list of actions you might take to make the situation more difficult.

In the face of fear, there are two possible options: Risk realizing it (without the desire to) or becoming aware of it so you can avoid it.

Only after you have identified your "false moves", can you begin to move in the right direction.

Discover how to use your emotional energy to your own advantage

It's clearer for you if I have explained it so far, and if the exercise you suggested has been tried.

Learning how to manage emotions is key to managing your inner impulses, which are more powerful than willpower.

You will need to get to grips with your emotions in order to learn how to harness it.

To be brave, we must face our fears.

You must endure the pain to get over it.

For anger to be channeled constructively,

Fear not your emotions. These emotions are not there to make you weaker, but rather to build you up.

I must mention, for my part, that in some instances, you may need a guided way to help you get rid of panic, anxiety and fears in a brief time using strategies tailored to your case.

Chapter 16: Steps for Attracting Health Wealth and Relationships

"What you believe, you can become." What you feel is what you attract. You create what your imagination allows you to. - Buddha

1) Attracting Health

You can improve your overall well-being or just one aspect of your health by paying attention to these things:

- Take control of your inner dialogue. Each emotion, thought, or feeling can have energetic consequences that can impact your body. If you constantly repeat to yourself, "I feel sadness", this can lead to stress and damage as well as increase cortisol or adrenaline levels in your body. You can imagine the long-term consequences of this behavior if you do it repeatedly.

Are you stuck in negative emotions like sadness or anger that send a negative message to your mind? Control your negative emotions. They can take over and sap your mental power.

- If your current treatment is for any condition, you should focus on how it will benefit you. Let's imagine that you are going through physical therapy to fix your bad knee. Instead of becoming passive and doing nothing, it's important to begin seeing the benefits and believing in the therapy.

- The subconscious mind controls how your body reacts to your thoughts. You can create more health if you put your focus on being healthy.

Steps:

i.e., ask for what you need.

iii. Each day, in front of your mirror, say to yourself, "I am healthy" and "My body is perfect in every aspect."

iii. Picture your body in perfect shape. Imagine yourself doing all the things your body is unable to do.

iv. For visual aids, make copies of pictures of healthy-looking people you admire and stick them to your mirror.

v. Be thankful and act as if your body is already healthy. A gratitude journal is a great way to increase your progress. Keep it open and note three things you are thankful for each day. The idea is to allow positive thoughts to sink in your subconscious and increase your awareness before you go to sleep.

- Read and listen to books about health.

For your health, here are some suggestions:

- "Healing powers flow through my body in every way."

- "I am fully healthy and full energy."

- "I care about my body and eat healthy, nutritious food."

- I am full of energy.

- "I'm getting stronger and better every day in everything."

"I love food and it loves me back,"

- "I am at my ideal body weight with a beautiful, healthy body."

2) Attracting wealth

Steps:

ii) Put emphasis on abundance thinking. Keep a gratitude journal. Write down one to three things you are grateful and spend a few minutes expressing gratitude. Remember that our subconscious holds the most weight when we feel the words. For example, you could write "I'm very grateful for my home," and then reflect on how amazing it is to have a lovely bed and hot shower.

iii. Your thoughts need to be aligned towards wealth. It won't work if there are opposing beliefs about wealth. I'm not going to be able or able to retire." You can't keep your mind from attracting wealth by thinking negative thoughts. You can stop these thoughts from coming up again.

iii. Identify your money blocks. You can do this by taking a look at your finances and writing down what you are going to do about them. Take a look at the list and decide what you're going to do.

iv. Write down your money targets on a piece, such as "I want to pay off my housing loan in 10 years", and keep it up-to-date.

v. Each day, focus on aligning yourself with wealth and abundance affirmations.

This is an example

- "I am fully open to prosperity, abundance in my own life."

"Money, a blessing." Every day I attract more cash."

- "I can attract wealth to myself."

- I am ready to receive unlimited wealth in the rest of my life.

- "Money flows to me, effortlessly.

3) Attracting and Maintaining Relationships

Your subconscious is like gravity. By focusing on the things you love, your subconscious will bring them into your lives. No matter how conscious or unconscious you make your reality, it will continue to give back more of the energy that you have released. To manifest love and joy, your frequencies should be tuned to your desires.

Steps:

ii) Let your subconscious know what type relationship you want. So that your subconscious is trained to search for the best path, be specific and deliberate about what you are looking to have in a partner. Instead of saying "Thanks," it might be "I'll have a partner who values family, is thoughtful, and gives" rather than "I feel lonely and alone." My workplace doesn't have a large enough dating pool. At this rate, I will never find my partner."

iii. Take steps to improve your self-esteem and personal transformation. Sometimes we need to change our behavior to be able to attract the things we desire. Also, it is important to align your vibrations to what you want. You must be thoughtful and giving if you desire to attract a giving and thoughtful partner.

iii. First, accept who you are. You should first improve your self-esteem. Insecurities can make you look weak and drive away partners. By radiating confidence and selfassurance, you can easily attract other people who are similar to you.

iv. Visualize, write and retell your story as vividly or as simply as possible to get your subconscious ready for new opportunities.

v. Don't obsess over your list and what you should expect. Be open-minded and willing to meet people who could be a match.

Tip: Do not focus on the unmet needs of your partner if you want to improve it. Remain grateful and appreciative of your partner and create positive vibrations that encourage joy and connectedness.

Chapter 17: Get rid of your fears

Sometimes it can be daunting to create abundance. Your biggest fears can often be confronted along the way. This chapter will address two of most common fears: the fear or failure and the fear or success. Although this may seem paradoxical at first, it is a fact of life. While some people are only afraid of one, others may be fearful of both. These fears can be a source of their inability and fearlessness in the future.

Fear of Failure

It is normal for us to want to be successful, but when this fear becomes a barrier to us engaging in productive activities toward achieving our goals, we face a major problem. You see, while we should all strive for success, putting too many of our efforts and commitments towards avoiding failure leads us to avoidant behavior. When you are unable to finish a task, you can give up.

This logic states that if your efforts are not too great, you shouldn't feel guilty about failing.

Not only do you have to fear the outcome of the failure you fear, but you also have to fear the possibility that you will fail. Instead of failing, your brain tells us to quit. Another common problem is giving in halfway through a journey after you experience the slightest setback.

Some ways the fear of failing manifests are:

The constant worry about what others might say about you failing is a constant habit. Because your thoughts become your reality, you start to believe that your failures are inevitable.

Every time you face a setback, you doubt your ability to succeed. Self-doubt is the biggest enemy of success. It makes you susceptible to negative thoughts.

You don't have to worry about what people think. Although we cannot all love each other, there are people who put so much effort into pleasing others that they don't have time to pursue their own goals. If this is a pattern you may be developing, it could indicate that you regard others' rejection as a failure.

You lower expectations. Your true goal is to create great success in your life and wealth. Then you decide that the bar is too high and you lower it. Before you know, you will settle to not losing your job or being able monthly to pay your bills. It is possible to be afraid that setting too high expectations will make it more difficult. You should lower your expectations if you are low in self-esteem.

Learn from your mistakes. You'll have noticed in my book that I have never mentioned the possibility of failing. Failing is part that is necessary for success. It's possible to fail many times before you finally reach your goal. Learn from your mistakes and ensure that you don't make the same mistakes again. It's often easy to see the faults in your past. It is possible to have problems with failure when you look back at a failed project.

You procrastinate. Procrastination is often associated with the fear and anxiety of failure. Procrastination causes people to become distracted by immediate satisfaction activities like scrolling social media, watching TV, or other menial tasks, instead of dedicating their time and energy to a specific goal.

The subconscious mind is responsible of these behaviors. Therefore, in order to conquer fear of failure, first identify the root cause. What makes you afraid to fail? What lessons, beliefs, and experiences have you had in life to help you become the person who fears failure? Perfectionism is often the culprit in many cases. Instead of looking at failure as an opportunity to learn, you should look at it in the context of a life that is otherwise perfect. The only way to overcome fear caused by perfectionionism is to realize that it is a myth and is holding you back. Failure is a part life. To become the victor you want to be, you must face it. Accepting failure as part success allows you to stop wasting energy running away. You understand that the rest of the world is beyond your control, so long as you do everything possible to succeed. Even the most successful people have failed at times in their pursuits. Their perseverance in the face of failure is what brought them their greatest success. You can overcome your fear by following these steps:

Take it with you

Fear of failure feeds on shame. You must learn to accept your role in success. These fears are usually suppressed within the conscious, and dwell in the subconscious. These fears can be overcome by expressing them and gaining control over your life.

Focus on the Things You Can Do

As powerful as visualizations, vision board, meditation and other methods can be to activate the law for attraction, you are ultimately not in control of what happens. The universe's power and mystery will grant you all the desires of your heart. Any attempt to exert control over it will be met with failure and disappointment. Recognize that your abilities are limited. Asking the universe for something will only give you so much. Keep going with your business as usual, making every effort to succeed. The rest, according to them, will take care.

Fear of success

Fear of success places you in a paradoxical place where you fear the very things you long for. The fear associated with success can be accompanied by a tendency to make things worse. It's not hard to see but can be challenging to identify and overcome. You must do this as it will help you to realize that all your hard work for abundance in life will go in vain if the things you do are not working. This section will talk about the causes, manifestations, solutions, and ways to overcome fear of success.

The causes

This is easy because the fear of success is caused by the desire for things not to change in the present moment. It is an insidious attempt not to change the status quo, to avoid upsetting people, or to take on more responsibilities. Fear of success is essentially a fear that your goals will come true. It also inflates negative outcomes.

If you are promoted and get rich, it will not only upset your peers but also cause friction in your friendships. If you want to disrupt your business's business model, you won't hesitate to launch a market-changing business product. There will be less time for leisure, more responsibilities, less family time. Even though you are motivated and driven, your subconscious mind can still be trapped in a world that has become familiar and comfortable. Success opens up a world of unknown possibilities and terrifying horrors. Why not stay right where you are?

Low self-esteem is another reason why people are afraid of success. Low self-esteem, which is a fundamental belief you are not worthy or worthy of success, can hinder your chances of succeeding. You should avoid toxic money beliefs like those discussed in Chapter 1. If you believe it is moral or unethical, you can't attract abundance in your own life.

Manifestation

The most common effect of fear is self-sabotage. In other words, people set themselves back and try to achieve less. When you are on track for achieving a specific goal, you'll be doing great. Then you do something that makes you go back to square 1. This only happens if your don't recognize the signs before it happens.

What are the signs of fear that you might not succeed? If you engage in more that two of the behaviors described below, you will realize you are hindering your true success. Why more than 2? Because it is possible to set a lower bar, work slowly, or feel low motivation. If they all occur at once, however, they can signal a larger problem.

* Set a less ambitious goal. Every goal starts with our thoughts. You may aim lower for reasons other than unreasonable goals. However, if you make it a habit and continue doing it even though it's impossible to accomplish the goal it could spell trouble.

* You don't feel enthusiastic. Your mind will do anything to keep you from succeeding if it is afraid of what you might experience. A

lack of motivation is just one way that the mind that is afraid is trying to stop success.

* You continually underachieve. Even though you know you can do more, you still consistently fail to deliver. You are holding your self back.

* You live with feelings of guilt, shame or envy. You envy others who have success and feel ashamed of your lack thereof. You are actively sabotaging you self.

* You aren't sure what you want. You have worked for years to achieve your goal. However, you are frustrated with yourself. You have doubted yourself and been envious, ashamed, and even embarrassed by your failures. It can reach the point where you aren't sure what you want anymore.

You can put an end to the fear of failure

There are a few ways you can overcome fear and achieve success. We'll be discussing five of these most effective.

Your Thoughts:

"Watch what you think," is something I mean literally and metaphorically. It is very helpful to notice the thoughts that come up when you picture a future of abundance. Your mind can help you to see the root cause of your fear. You can then address the root issues and improve your chances to succeed. Your thoughts should be positive. This can easily be achieved through mindfulness and gratitude journals.

Meditation

Meditation allows you to tap into the deepest, most darkest parts your soul and tune it towards success. Mindfulness meditation can really help you to identify and overcome your fear of failure or self-sabotage. You can use it to reverse the cycle and envision a world that is full of abundance. Your brain will stop fighting you for success by normalizing it through visualization.

Start a Success library

Sometimes we fear success because we don't trust ourselves enough to accomplish our goals. One way to regain your faith in your ability is by listing all the remarkable things you have done. Inspiring quotes, articles, and success stories are also possible. These will help you to overcome your fear of success when it strikes.

Look Around You

Even if the things you do are hindering your success chances, it is likely that your current circumstances are not very good. This is a great way of getting back on track to your success.

Mantras

When you have negative beliefs about yourself and fear of success, mantras can be very powerful. If you can think of positive phrases that you can repeat over and over until your subconscious mind begins to believe them and then gets out of your way. This combination of positive intonations and Buddhist mantra chants will help you increase your vibrations to attract your abundance.

Chapter 18: Death is inevitable

People find it hard to accept the reality of their death. This is something that many people do not accept. It is mostly because they associate death as fear or pain. Fear because they don't know what or when they will die. There is also pain, as they associate death and loss with their loved ones.

However, it is evident that those who accept this fact will do better with their lives than those that don't. You begin to see the value in every moment, and you live your life more intentionally.

If you're looking for a way to figure out what your life is about, it might be a good idea to reflect on what you want people remember you by, how you want them to see you, and what experience you'd like to have before they do. Although this doesn't diminish fear, it helps you live more fully by enjoying every moment. It doesn't matter how old or young you are; you do not have the luxury and time to enjoy every moment of your life.

Time is a finite precious resource. This isn't a dress rehearsal. Go after your dreams and tell people that you love them. Never let anyone tell or convince you that it's impossible to live the life of your dreams. Don't wait for tomorrow to do what you could today.

The best place to start if you want to live life to the fullest is to learn about time management. Time management can be described as the systematic planning and utilization of one's time to its best. Time management allows you to achieve even the most ambitious goals, while still allowing for time to have fun and enjoy your family and friends. True fulfillment is not only about making money. It's also about being able to prioritize the things that matter to you, while still striving for your goals.

Manage your Time

You must manage your time. Your time is precious. Your time is finite, so you need to manage it.

You can do more in less time when you manage your time.

Your time management skills will improve your decision making.

You can make more of your time by planning for it and making better use of it.

You will be more successful if your time is managed well.

Time management reduces stress and overwhelm.

Time management is about discipline. This is especially true if you're able to follow your time management plan.

Management of your time will allow you to enjoy your spare time.

How to Manage Your Time

There are many time-management resources on the market, but there are some general principles to managing your time. Let's discuss them. It is possible to get the best out of time management by taking time to monitor what you do. This will allow you to see where your time is going and give you a better understanding of how it is being used. Knowledge is power. By understanding your body rhythms, when you are most active, as well as how long they take, you will be better equipped to recognize the things that you don't need and eliminate them.

Notify your brain if you are unsure of what to do. Your brain is limited by how many things it can remember in a short time. Other activities may overwhelm you, and you might forget some. Some people prefer having a master list of tasks that lists everything they need to do. Later, when creating daily or weekly plans you will be able to refer back to your task list and divide the tasks.

There is a constant debate over whether a daily or weekly planner is more effective. You can also assign certain activities to certain days using a weekly planner. You could, for instance, assign creative tasks on Mondays, Wednesdays, or Fridays. Also, you could schedule meetings on Tuesdays and Thurdays. However, you could also allocate specific hours for these tasks throughout your workday, such as mornings and afternoons for creative projects, meetings or spontaneous activities, and even set aside time for them. Pick one, try it out, then discard it.

Prioritize your tasks. You can do this best by using the 80/20 principle. This principle states 80 percent is usually achieved by 20 percent of efforts. Although this percentage could fluctuate, it's generally agreed that certain activities can be more heavy than others. Because these activities require the most effort, it is essential to determine which ones are most likely to be the most weighty.

These tasks can be done first so that you don't have to do them later. You will learn more about prioritization at the end of this chapter.

You must learn to delegate. There are tasks that you can do quicker and more efficiently than others. Spending too much time on tasks can cause exhaustion and make it difficult to focus on more important tasks. Fear of delegating is one reason people avoid it. Perfectionists often feel that no one can complete the task as well. But this is a recipe in disaster. If you require a task to be done in a certain manner, it is okay to give instructions. Once you have given the task, make sure to assign it to someone who can do it well. For tasks that you don't enjoy doing but that you know you can leave to someone else, delegation is a good option.

Avoid multitasking. Multitasking is tempting because you think it will speed up your job. It may seem like this is true. But you'll often find that you don't perform the task as well when you take the time to concentrate on one task at once. If you focus on one task at time, it is easier to become in a flow mode, which can be where new ideas emerge and increase your ability to learn and comprehend. Once you have set a time limit for the task, commit to working on it until completion or until the time expires.

Avoid over-planning. Your day may not go exactly according to your plan. Be prepared for interruptions and distractions. Your boss may assign you a task, or you may get a client. If you don't do the task as promised, your boss will. This is what you are wasting your time. It is best to assign only 1-3 key tasks per day. This is important to ensure you give them the most effort and attention. Furthermore, it decreases the feeling overwhelm that you feel when you have a lot of things to do. It would be easier to add tasks from your master to-do list to your task list, rather than waiting for them to be completed. Relaxation and leisure should be planned.

Develop a Sense of Urgency

Once you have decided how to organize your tasks and which time management strategy works best for you then it is best that you create an urgency to reach your goals. It's because you don't know how long you have until you reach your goal. Second, it will keep you motivated. In order to generate creativity and innovation, a sense of urgency is a great way to foster creativity. A sense of urgency increases productivity and can help you build momentum. It is important to take initiative in pursuing your dreams and developing a sense urgency. The following strategies will help create a sense o urgency.

Make sure you break down your goals in short-term and longer-term milestones. You should also set deadlines to let you know when it is time to move.

Develop a competitive spirit. It is easier to be competitive when you know there are others who are pursuing similar goals to you.

You can create your own deadlines. A deadline is a great way to overcome procrastination.

Value your time. Value each moment. This will reduce the temptation to waste time and make it more valuable.

It is better to value long-term rewards and pleasure than instant gratification. You may enjoy binging your favorite shows now, but a successful business will bring you joy for much longer.

You can create an inspiring vision. It should be challenging and motivating. It is important to have a challenging vision so you can feel accomplished when it is achieved.

Establish momentum. It is much harder to build momentum than it is to maintain it. You'll want the momentum to continue building on your gains.

Prioritization

Prioritizing helps you differentiate between tasks that you must focus on and those that you are not. Prioritizing should be based on how important and urgent the tasks are. The most important and urgent tasks are those that require immediate attention and must be completed quickly. Some tasks, like doing laundry or mowing lawn, are not necessary but can be delegated. Avoidance of tasks that are not important or urgent is better than doing them later. You should put your primary focus on tasks that are important but not urgent. Here you will find all your daily tasks related your goals.

Prioritization allows to you concentrate your time and energy on the tasks that are most important. People who prioritize their time often discover that they achieve more in a shorter amount of time. Prioritization can also mean being selective about who you keep around. You will be happier, less stressed, and have more fun with people who support you. Prioritize the work that you enjoy. This is a good way to combat procrastination. We tend to procrastinate over tasks we do not love. Although you'll have to give up your comfort and time to pursue your goals you will feel successful.

We may not have the time that we would like to spend on the things we desire, but that is no reason for us to panic. No matter your age, your circumstances or background, you may find that you do not have to work very hard to reach your goals. It might mean we are busy for a while, but it is not a bad thing. If you want your goals to be achieved, be ready to prioritize and to create a sense if urgency. We all have the same 24-hour day. Those who manage it well achieve more than those with less.

Are there dreams you'd like to realize but haven't been able to accomplish? How can I better manage my time so that I am able to accomplish more? Sometimes it is as easy to maximize your time, even if it is only five minutes. You'll see yourself progressing towards your goals little by little.

Conclusion

Manifesting can be difficult at the beginning. Consistent practice will help you overcome your negative feelings and take control. Eventually, manifesting will be second nature.

Manifesting means that your thoughts turn into reality. It is essential to remain positive in your thinking and focus on what you want. This can help attract the opportunities that you long for.

Now it is up to you believe in manifestation, to learn the techniques, as well as to make use of it to your benefit. You can use the Law of Attraction to attract health, love wealth, happiness and joy in a positive manner. I encourage you to look at what the Law of Attraction has to offer. It will bring you happiness.

These are simple steps to follow in order to achieve your goals.

Write positive affirmations, and have them read every day

Focus on your desires

Visualize

Believe that the universe has granted you your desires.

Keep a Gratitude Journal. It can be used to track what you are thankful for.

Be positive to beat the negativity

Repeat the procedure to reprogram your subconscious mind

Final note: When your thoughts and feelings are filled with positive vibes, it will be easier to attract positive energy into your life. Don't be afraid to pursue the life you want.

www.ingramcontent.com/pod-product-compliance
Lightning Source LLC
Chambersburg PA
CBHW050406120526
44590CB00015B/1843